Historical Fiction Clubs

Lucy Calkins and Mary Ehrenworth

Photography by Peter Cunningham

Illustrations by Marjorie Martinelli

HEINEMANN ◆ PORTSMOUTH, NH

To Ali Marron, with thanks for it all.—Lucy and Mary

Heinemann
361 Hanover Street
Portsmouth, NH 03801–3912
www.heinemann.com

Offices and agents throughout the world

The authors and publisher wish to thank those who have generously given permission to reprint borrowed material:

Rose Blanche, by Roberto Innocenti. © Creative Editions is an imprint of The Creative Company, Mankato, MN.

The Tiger Rising. Copyright © 2001 by Kate DiCamillo. Reproduced by permission of the publisher, Candlewick Press.

From *Out of the Dust*, by Karen Hesse. Copyright © 1997 by Karen Hesse. Reprinted by permission of Scholastic, Inc.

Cataloging-in-Publication data is on file with the Library of Congress.

ISBN-13: 978-0-325-07718-5

Series editorial team: Anna Gratz Cockerille, Karen Kawaguchi, Tracy Wells, Felicia O'Brien, Debra Doorack, Jean Lawler, Marielle Palombo, and Sue Paro
Production: Elizabeth Valway, David Stirling, and Abigail Heim
Cover and interior designs: Jenny Jensen Greenleaf
Photography: Peter Cunningham
Illustrations: Marjorie Martinelli
Composition: Publishers' Design and Production Services, Inc.
Manufacturing: Steve Bernier

Printed in the United States of America on acid-free paper
19 18 17 16 15 EBM 1 2 3 4 5

Acknowledgments

THIS UNIT is such a favorite at the Teachers College Reading and Writing Project that many people have added their input over years and years of teaching it. How thankful we are for Kathleen Tolan's wisdom about the intersection of book clubs and guided reading groups and about teaching towards agency. We're grateful for Kelly Boland Hohne's astute attention to skill progressions, especially those that apply to interpretive and analytic reading. We're grateful to Audra Robb and Ali Marron for their work with interpretation and performance assessments. Emily Butler Smith has been invaluable with learning progressions, Shana Frazin with literature, Marjorie Martinelli and Liz Dunford with charts, and Julia Mooney with all things. Kelly Wynne, one of the graduate students in the Literacy Specialist program, functioned as a research assistant, and we are eternally grateful to her. So many people, so many helping hands! Perhaps none more so than my assistant, Mary Ann Mustac, who has become an editor along the way.

Because this unit has been taught for years and has been central to many of our summer institutes, and because it was written as an overly brimful book years ago, the challenge when writing this was that of selection and design. We wanted to make the unit accessible and to be sure that it accelerated kids' progress along the progressions that undergird the unit. We therefore spent a lot of time thinking between work on accelerating kids' progress up levels of text complexity, on the intersection of nonfiction and fiction, and on writing about reading, trying to put just the best work forward.

That process involved lots of drafts and lots of work, trying to carve the lion out of the stone. In that process, our editor, Karen Kawaguchi, was absolutely invaluable. Karen has been a senior editor on Units of Study books for a while now, and she grasps the design of minilessons, small-group work, units, and curriculum. She is also an exacting wordsmith, and one who knows how to write spare, clean prose. Karen helped us do that ever-so-hard work of "killing our darlings." She was assisted by Anna Gratz Cockerille, who managed the comings and goings, kept the pipeline moving, and was a coordinator of the effort. Thanks for that support.

Meanwhile we couldn't be more grateful to the team at Heinemann. The leadership team there is a joy to partner with: Vicki Boyd, Stephen Perepeluk, and Abby Heim. The timeframe on these books was extremely tight, and this particular book caused extra work, extra delays. Abby Heim and David Stirling and the rest of the team took it—and us—in stride, and for that we are eternally grateful.

—Lucy and Mary

Contents

BEND III The Intersection of Historical Fiction and History

An Orientation to the Unit

ALTHOUGH YOU KNOW that this is a unit on reading skills—specifically on developing ideas about characters, determining themes, inferring within a text, comparing and contrasting texts, synthesizing across texts, and talking and writing about reading—for your kids, this is a unit on historical fiction. And that, in and of itself, will get their blood pumping.

When reading historical fiction, the novels themselves are inherently complex. The characters inevitably live in places in which our students have not lived, in times they have not known. The reader must figure out the nature of the setting, the ways people live, and not just who the characters are but also the relationships the characters have to historical tensions. So, the reading work will be appropriately intense.

The reading is especially important, too, because the stories are often ones that tell of a young person struggling towards social justice. Whether it is a young girl struggling to assert her independence against the backdrop of the Dust Bowl or two boys struggling to cross the color line during a civil rights movement they don't yet understand, the stories illuminate themes of cruelty and courage, power and resistance. You'll see your children realize during this unit that reading is, really, about learning how to live.

Because the work of this unit is demanding, we begin right from the start to channel readers to work within same-book clubs. And because historical fiction requires readers to come to learn about a time and place in history—because background knowledge enriches the reading exponentially—we suggest each club adopt a time period and read several historical fiction novels, as well as nonfiction related to that time period. This requires some careful work provisioning your classroom, and there are compromises you can and cannot make if you have limited books, so please be sure to read the Getting Ready section at the end of this orientation.

There are three bends within this unit. The first bend equips students with the skills they need to handle increasingly complex texts in general. When kids were younger, they needed to be able to read a part of the text while still keeping in mind the pages that came before it (aware of how the current page related to the earlier material), while simultaneously predicting pages to come. Keeping all the parts of the unfolding storyline in mind while reading was the really big challenge. As your students approach the end of fourth grade and the start of fifth, their books will become increasingly complex, and they'll be asked to juggle more balls (only really, it's more timelines!). For example, while the timeline of a story—say, *Number the Stars*, the demonstration text for this unit—is unfolding, readers need to be aware that the historical timeline of the Holocaust is also unfolding, and that those two timelines intersect. Then, too, new characters enter the drama, and sometimes there is a secondary story around one of them. Children learn there is a sister, now dead, and her boyfriend, off stage most of the time, but carrying on his own subplot.

In Bend I, then, you'll help readers to synthesize the evolving settings with the plotlines and subplots of whatever texts they are reading. You'll also teach them how to construct a sense of the setting not just as a physical place, but as an emotional place as well, and in doing so, to read with increased attention to the mood in the text.

Bend II of this unit shines a light on interpretation, helping students to engage in this ambitious intellectual work. This bend embarks upon the heady intellectual work of interpretation, building on that which you began in Unit 1, *Interpreting Characters: The Heart of the Story*. As the stories your children are reading become more complicated, one of the most important things you'll teach is that their novels are not just about what is happening—the books are not just about the plots. Their novels are about ideas, and as readers, it is their job to draft and revise their sense of those ideas. Your goal is *not* that your students learn to articulate the ideas *you* already have about a book, nor that they somehow stumble upon a theme which seems to you to be "right." Your goal, instead, is for your readers to learn to draft and revise and elaborate upon possible interpretations of a text as they read and as they discuss books with each other. You won't tell students "the theme" of a book, or send them off to seek evidence for an idea they did not develop themselves. All of this work with your students will happen first within one text they are reading, then across texts, and then finally between texts and their lives.

Bend III of the unit brings in nonfiction texts and invites readers to think between those texts and the stories they are reading. Students learn to stuff historical documents into the pages of their historical fiction novels, and to read between those novels and the relevant nonfiction texts. They also learn to think about how the information they are learning enlarges their understanding of the characters, their struggles, their perspectives, their insights, and their knowledge of history. In this bend, students will call on their strategies for reading nonfiction, striving to both glean knowledge and apply that knowledge to other texts. There's a strong cross-text emphasis at the end of the unit, with children being asked to think across fiction and nonfiction, across story and history, and across the books they have read now and in the past, and their own life.

SUPPORTING SKILL PROGRESSIONS

This unit, like the first unit of your year, supports your fourth-graders in learning to read in ways that allow them to make deep, rich interpretations and to engage in strong, analytic reading.

Your children will probably embark on this unit in the spring of fourth grade. For many readers, this marks a period of growth not only in understanding and knowledge but also in independence. Before embarking on this unit, you will want to read the Narrative Reading Learning Progression for fourth grade, so that you can help your children set clear goals. You'll also want to review those for third grade as your conferring and small-group work may need to shore up foundational skills on the third-grade progression, even while your unit advances into the work of fourth grade. If you have many strong and experienced readers, you may want to glimpse ahead to the fifth-grade progression as well.

By the spring of fourth grade, the novels that your students are reading become denser, and they pose some interesting new challenges. Students who read these more challenging texts will need to be ready to embrace complexity in comprehension as well as interpretation. There will be more characters to

keep track of, more plotlines to follow, more nuanced settings to make sense of. The stories they are reading will also develop more than one theme. It's going to be important that your fourth-graders learn to welcome these challenges, and develop reading practices that help them attend to everything that is unfolding in their novels.

This need to tackle the challenges of their books and read more deeply crosses over to more than just the "Determining Themes/Cohesion" strand. This unit supports essential character skills, and you'll see that the "Character Response/Change" thread invites students to not only identify character change but also notice why characters act the way they do, including what causes change. Students are expected to recognize that characters are complicated—work that relates to the thread "Character Traits." In addition to being able to infer about characters, though, they need to think about multiple possible reasons for why changes might occur in a story.

When looking at expectations for third-graders versus fourth-graders, note that fourth-graders are expected to be aware that there is no one simple cause for a character or a place to change—and the causes may be subtle. The causes of change may come from any one of the story elements—from other characters, from relationships, from the plotline, yes, but also from the setting. Thinking deeply about why things change in a story involves thinking also about how different characters react to situations and deal with challenges and grow insight. All of this intellectual work is related to the expectations in the strand, "Inferring About Characters and Other Story Elements."

As mentioned in the first unit, thinking deeply about a story begins when readers are *orienting* themselves to a text. Especially in this unit, students must begin reading, aware that the fact that they are reading historical fiction already clues them into some kinds of details that will be important in the story. It will be important for them to learn about the times, and to notice, especially, if trouble is brewing, as it generally is in the settings for historical fiction stories. They'll need to notice that the characters probably belong to different social groups, play different roles, in the society of the story, and understanding the interaction of setting, characters, and plots will involve thinking about why characters react to events and to changes in the setting as they do.

The interesting thing is that because the stories your children are reading are increasingly complex, they'll have a fair amount of work to do just to establish literal comprehension of the text. The strand "Envisioning/Predicting"—making mental movies—is newly challenging when the stories are set

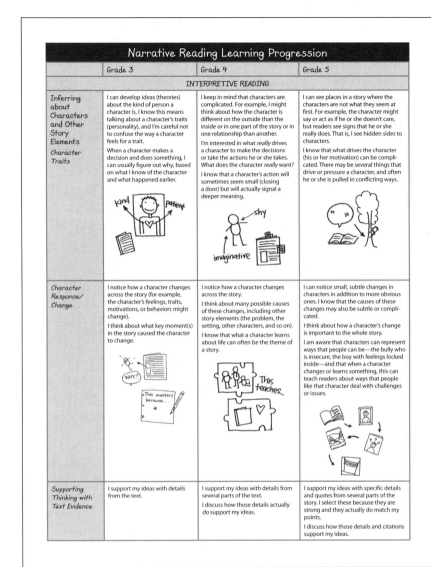

Narrative Reading Learning Progression

	Grade 3	Grade 4	Grade 5
INTERPRETIVE READING			
Inferring about Characters and Other Story Elements *Character Traits*	I can develop ideas (theories) about the kind of person a character is. I know this means talking about a character's traits (personality), and I'm careful not to confuse the way a character feels for a trait. When a character makes a decision and does something, I can usually figure out why, based on what I know of the character and what happened earlier.	I keep in mind that characters are complicated. For example, I might think about how the character is different on the outside than the inside or in one part of the story or in one relationship than another. I'm interested in what *really* drives a character to make the decisions or take the actions he or she takes. What does the character *really* want? I know that a character's action will sometimes seem small (closing a door) but will actually signal a deeper meaning.	I can see places in a story where the characters are not what they seem at first. For example, the character might say or act as if he or she doesn't care, but readers see signs that he or she really does. That is, I see hidden sides to characters. I know that what drives the character (his or her motivation) can be complicated. There may be several things that drive or pressure a character, and often he or she is pulled in conflicting ways.
Character Response/ Change	I notice how a character changes across the story (for example, the character's feelings, traits, motivations, or behaviors might change). I think about what key moment(s) in the story caused the character to change.	I notice how a character changes across the story. I think about many possible causes of these changes, including other story elements (the problem, the setting, other characters, and so on). I know that what a character learns about life can often be the theme of a story.	I can notice small, subtle changes in characters in addition to more obvious ones. I know that the causes of these changes may also be subtle or complicated. I think about how a character's change is important to the whole story. I am aware that characters can represent ways that people can be—the bully who is insecure, the boy with feelings locked inside—and that when a character changes or learns something, this can teach readers about ways that people like that character deal with challenges or issues.
Supporting Thinking with Text Evidence	I support my ideas with details from the text.	I support my ideas with details from several parts of the text. I discuss how those details actually *do* support my ideas.	I support my ideas with specific details and quotes from several parts of the story. I select these because they are strong and they actually do match my points. I discuss how those details and citations support my ideas.

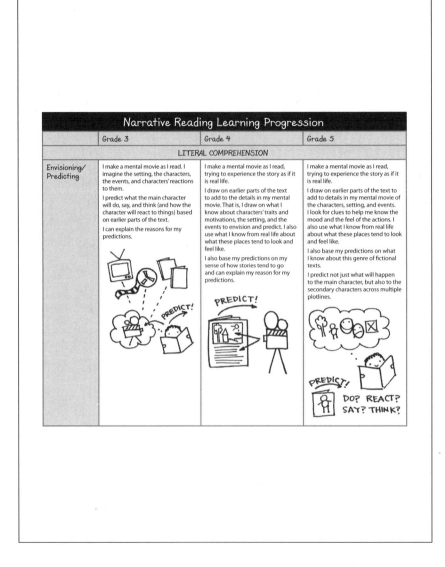

Narrative Reading Learning Progression

	Grade 3	Grade 4	Grade 5
LITERAL COMPREHENSION			
Envisioning/ Predicting	I make a mental movie as I read. I imagine the setting, the characters, the events, and characters' reactions to them. I predict what the main character will do, say, and think (and how the character will react to things) based on earlier parts of the text. I can explain the reasons for my predictions.	I make a mental movie as I read, trying to experience the story as if it is real life. I draw on earlier parts of the text to add to the details in my mental movie. That is, I draw on what I know about characters' traits and motivations, the setting, and the events to envision and predict. I also use what I know from real life about what these places tend to look and feel like. I also base my predictions on my sense of how stories tend to go and can explain my reason for my predictions.	I make a mental movie as I read, trying to experience the story as if it is real life. I draw on earlier parts of the text to add to details in my mental movie of the characters, setting, and events. I look for clues to help me know the mood and the feel of the actions. I also use what I know from real life about what these places tend to look and feel like. I also base my predictions on what I know about this genre of fictional texts. I predict not just what will happen to the main character, but also to the secondary characters across multiple plotlines.

in worlds that students need to construct, piece by piece through reading. This work will also help students to meet and exceed the expectations in the Reading: Literature (RL) strand of the Common Core State Standards (CCSS), RL 4.3, which expects that students will be able to describe in depth not only characters but also setting and events.

Of course, the "Monitoring for Sense" strand becomes more important, too. A character says or does something out of the ordinary, or the timeframe seems to have changed, and readers need to think, "Huh? How is that happening? Did I miss something?" and then readers need to reread, using fix-up strategies to regain a grip on how the pieces of the story are fitting together.

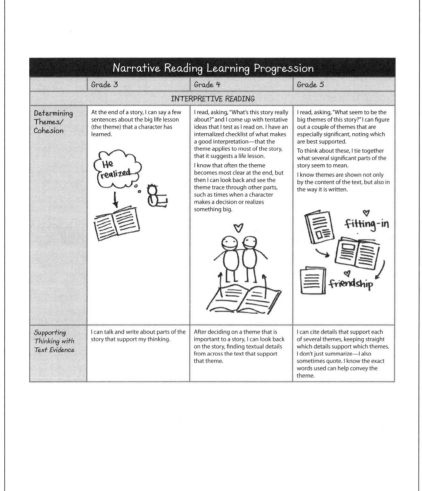

Narrative Reading Learning Progression			
	Grade 3	Grade 4	Grade 5
INTERPRETIVE READING			
Determining Themes/ Cohesion	At the end of a story, I can say a few sentences about the big life lesson (the theme) that a character has learned.	I read, asking, "What's this story really about?" and I come up with tentative ideas that I test as I read on. I have an internalized checklist of what makes a good interpretation—that the theme applies to most of the story, that it suggests a life lesson. I know that often the theme becomes most clear at the end, but then I can look back and see the theme trace through other parts, such as times when a character makes a decision or realizes something big.	I read, asking, "What seem to be the big themes of this story?" I can figure out a couple of themes that are especially significant, noting which are best supported. To think about these, I tie together what several significant parts of the story seem to mean. I know themes are shown not only by the content of the text, but also in the way it is written.
Supporting Thinking with Text Evidence	I can talk and write about parts of the story that support my thinking.	After deciding on a theme that is important to a story, I can look back on the story, finding textual details from across the text that support that theme.	I can cite details that support each of several themes, keeping straight which details support which themes. I don't just summarize—I also sometimes quote. I know the exact words used can help convey the theme.

As texts contain more flashbacks and flash-forwards, more gaps in time, and different perspectives and places, monitoring for sense becomes increasingly necessary. Paying careful attention to the "Story Elements: Time, Plot, Setting" thread will be critical.

Another strand to which this work will relate is "Word Work" including the Building Vocabulary thread. Expect that as your students read more challenging texts, students will need to return to work in "Word Work" and "Fluency" and learn how to apply those skills to more difficult texts. Building vocabulary work in this unit will involve students continuing to build a knowledge base of literary language; however, as they read historical fiction, they will develop a vocabulary that relates to the time periods about which they are reading.

One phenomenon you'll notice is that in both writing and reading, work that is at first done late in the process (during revision in writing, and at the story's end in reading) often moves forward in the process once learners become more skilled. Your students should, by now, begin to read interpretively even when they are in the early chapters of a novel. "Hmmm, I'm wondering what this story is starting to be about?' they think, and they generate possible ideas and read on, looking at the text through the lens of those ideas. This expectation is detailed within the "Determining Themes/Cohesion" strand of the Narrative Reading Learning Progression. Fourth-graders are expected to read and from the start be asking, "What's this story really about?" This is also an expectation of fourth-graders by the Common Core State Standards (RL 4.2)—and virtually all state standards—which expect students to be able to "determine a theme of a story, drama, or poem from details in the text." Remember that fourth-graders are expected to pay attention to the details and connect more of them on the run, in addition to being able to look back and trace a theme through different parts of the story. The first fiction unit began this work, and this unit will take up and extend this work even further. Next year, students will be expected to consider multiple possible themes, and this unit will set students up for that ambitious work.

Then, too, as students get stronger at reading one text deeply, they'll be expected to take that work into the work of the strand, "Comparing and Contrasting Story Elements and Themes." At this level, there is an expectation that students will be able to take two stories that are working to convey a similar theme and be able to consider how that theme might be slightly different in each of those stories. And, they'll need to ask, "How is it developed differently?"

In addition to major expectations for students in inferring and interpretation, there are also major expectations for them in the area of analytic reading. Remember that in the first unit, students were engaged in work in "Analyzing Parts of a Story in Relation to the Whole." In third grade, your students learned to think of their novels in terms of story structure, noticing the portion of the book where the author introduces the characters and lets readers know the character's motivations and traits, and the parts of the book where the problem is clarified, intensified, and resolved. By fourth grade, your students will continue to ponder why the author included certain parts—and the reasons have to do with author's craft or story elements. In historical fiction, for instance, you'll lead your readers to think hard about how and why certain parts of the story develop the setting, as the historical setting has such a profound impact on characters.

This unit will continue that work, and in addition, it will offer more work around "Analyzing Author's Craft." When studying author's craft, students will need to continue the work they began in third grade of noticing when

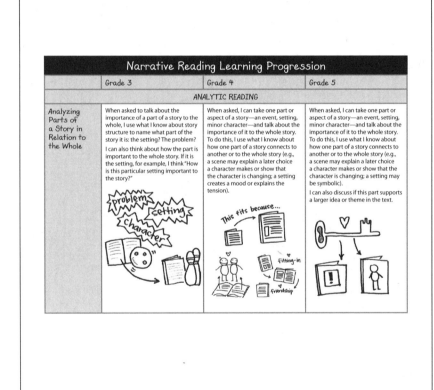

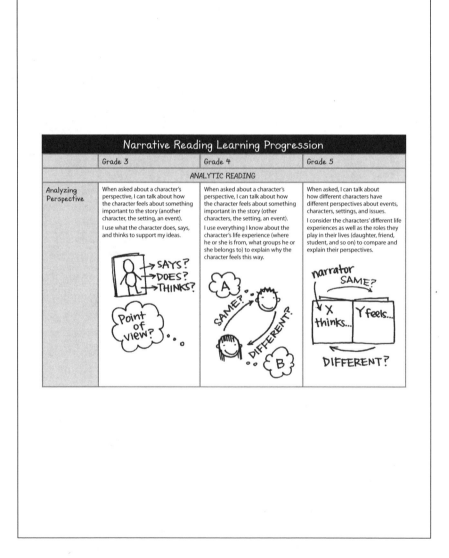

an author has done something that stands out and asking the all-important question, "Why might the author have done that?" They'll be expected to study word choice carefully, work that will relate to the "Word Work" strand, as authors begin to play more with figurative language. And, they'll need to consider how specific word choices and other craft choices relate to theme(s).

Students will also be expected to ramp up their work in "Analyzing Perspective." Earlier this year, students will have learned to identify the point of view in texts—is this a story told in first person? Is this a story told in third person? In this unit, they learn to think about perspective, noticing that the way a character sees the world and responds to an event reflects that character's role, age, religion, and group membership as much as the character's personality. This work will also help students meet the expectations of many state standards. In this unit, students also consider which perspectives are missing. Which character's voices and thoughts are we *not* hearing?

A final major expectation, one that is particularly essential to this unit, is in "Critical Reading." As in all units, you should expect to see students improve in the "Growing Ideas" thread, learning to raise their own questions. And, as this unit moves on, you'll want to see students reading critically. Readers can see with what issues a text is dealing, and ask, "Do I agree?" They can ask whose voices are heard and whose are silent. They can consider the experiences of different groups in the past and how that relates to power in the present. Students work in texts needs to be more than just taking in what a text says. Students need to be critical, active, questioning—asking if they agree with what a text is trying to say and wondering about the implications for how to live differently today.

OVERVIEW

This unit is organized so that children read in the company of friends, reading shared historical fiction from a particular era with support from a book club. Your readers will have participated in clubs earlier, and will relish a chance to return to this social structure. Clubs are important because it is helpful for young people to develop interpretations in the company of others. If the real goal here is to help kids' author lives in which reading matters, then it is essential that kids experience the shared pleasure of reading with friends.

Bend I: Tackling Complex Texts

The first bend teaches readers to read complex texts with strong literal comprehension, monitoring for sense, actively working to fit the pieces together, and working with support from a book club to keep track of multiple plotlines, many characters, and shifts in time and place.

Historical fiction, at the levels at which your children are probably reading, moves swiftly. Readers need to gather a lot of information quickly, so details matter. If you learn something on the second page or in the first chapter, it's because you're going to need it later in the story. And so you'll teach your readers to accumulate details. Essential reading tools, such as timelines, graphic organizers, and lists of characters, which your readers may not have needed for a time, now become important tools again. This is important, because one thing you'll be teaching here is that good readers don't wait for a teacher to tell them how to use their comprehension strategies. Strong readers know that, as their books get harder, they have to work harder—and they know how to do this.

In the first session, you'll invite—even entice—your children into the world of historical fiction. Then you immerse them in figuring out when and where the story is taking place and *what kind of* place it is. You'll help your students grasp that setting is intimately related to atmosphere and mood and to be alert to both the emotional and the physical setting. You'll say, "Readers pay attention to mood and atmosphere of the places in which stories are set. They realize that the story will almost never say 'this shows that trouble is brewing' or 'this shows a sense of hope,' so you must assemble clues to figure out what kind of place this is." This work is important in most high-stakes assessments and is a big part of comprehending most complex stories. It's both the work of analyzing part of the text in relation to the whole and of noticing author's craft and its effect on the story.

Then, too, you'll be getting your students into clubs right off the bat, leading them to create a constitution for their club and beginning to build a club identity. Clubs require children to work collaboratively, meaning they need to learn to compromise, share power, and negotiate. In this unit, students will be tackling complex texts and doing more sophisticated thinking. To do that well, you'll guide them to commit to taking care of their club, which involves listening to *every* member and remembering what active listening really looks and sounds like.

By giving each club a chance to construct its own identity, you also give yourself a way to help a club tackle the work of reading more closely, more actively, than ever before. The club's agenda will be collaboratively shaped by you and the club members. Based on your assessments of the readers in a club, you steer one club to seize upon the notion that they could do tons of drama, aiming to act out and experience the books they're reading, meanwhile helping to develop their fluency. Another club could decide to read more slowly, to do more rereading and more writing about reading. You could help these club members develop their ability to read analytically and closely. All club members will need to learn ways to talk and write more thoughtfully and with increasing independence. Fortunately, the books themselves make this work imperative.

In the first chapters of a complex novel, there is so much new information coming at readers that it's important to gather all the story essentials—the who, what, where, when, why—as if tacking these elements up onto a bulletin board. Strong readers accumulate information about the topics and the people that thread through a text.

To keep track of all this information, you will let students know that in historical fiction, stories unfold along two timelines, not one. Readers need to be aware of both timelines—for historical events and for the protagonist's life—and then must examine the relationships *between* those timelines. You'll guide students to ask, "How does history influence the big events in the protagonist's life?" Another day, you'll teach students to step into their characters' shoes and realize that the characters are shaped by the times in which they live. They will learn to ask, "Who is telling the story? Whose point of view does the reader get when reading this book?"

Constructing a coherent storyline becomes challenging in these historical fiction texts, because more complex stories have multiple plotlines, back stories, characters who are not what they seem, and problems that remain unsolved. Keeping the story chronology straight is especially challenging in complex texts because jumps in time are often not well-marked. Characters also experience pressures from many sources. You will want your students to think hard about what influences a character's thoughts and decisions, about how the character's role and place in history shapes his or her actions. This work involves the skill of analyzing perspective, and you'll use that strand in the Narrative Reading Learning Progression to support your students in this tricky work.

Bend II: Interpreting Complex Texts

The second bend embarks upon the heady intellectual work of interpretation. As the stories your children are reading become more complicated, one of the most important things you'll teach is that their novels are not just about what is happening—the books are not just about the plots. Their novels are about ideas.

Moreover, their books will be about *more than one idea*. This is new work for a lot of readers, especially young readers who came of age searching for one big idea of a text—often one that is revealed at the end of the story. You'll counteract that limited understanding by teaching your students that reading is about drafting and revising ideas. You'll do this work with your students first within one text, then across texts, and then between texts and their lives. You'll teach kids to grow nuanced ideas and to read in order to be changed by the new worlds and characters they encounter.

Our goal is that your students learn to articulate significant ideas about their books, to revise those ideas on their own, and to reconsider and elaborate those ideas in the company of other readers. Their club work will be tremendously important here, as kids learn that their ideas are more powerful in coalition than when they work alone. You'll teach students to prepare ideas for their club meetings, and then help them use their club conversations to build on each other's ideas rather than jumping from topic to topic. Indeed, one of this unit's most significant lessons, and we hope one of the most lasting, will be teaching children that their greatest strength lies in sharing ideas with each other.

You'll teach students that strong readers read complex texts alertly, poised to recognize when a passage is significant. You will teach children to pause especially at passages that, as you'll put it, "seem to be written in bold letters," then to think about how this passage connects to other parts of the text, and then to figure out what it is *really* saying. Your students might notice if an image or a word is repeated often, wondering if it might be a symbol of something bigger, or they might notice if something catches them by surprise and stands out, thinking, "Why might the author have put in this surprising part?"

You will also help them understand more about symbolism. When a person has something huge, complex, and deep to say, often the most powerful way to convey that meaning is through tiny, concrete specifics. In turn, when readers think or write about big ideas from a book, they support their ideas with small moments, small details, and small objects found in the text. In

Number the Stars, the star necklace, imprinted on Annemarie's hand, is not just a necklace. That Star of David is a tiny thing—yet so big. Exploring the meaning of that imprint on her hand will be a way to bring children toward a study of symbolism and of abstraction—and of the relationship between gritty specifics and big ideas. You'll use the "Determining Themes/Cohesion" strand of the Narrative Reading Learning Progression to check students' progress toward developing these skills, teaching that one way readers tackle this work is to have in mind an internalized sense of the qualities of strong thematic interpretations.

You'll also remind students that when readers have developed an interpretation of a book, they keep it in mind, using it like a lens, growing and shaping that interpretation as they read on. You are likely to find that once you rally students around the importance of growing interpretations of a text, they may hold so doggedly to their interpretations that their thinking stalls—and sometimes they ignore parts of the story that don't fit their interpretation. You'll want to address this head-on, directly teaching your readers that their initial idea will change. Perhaps they'll add a *because* statement to their idea, or make that idea more precise or broader. Perhaps their conversations with others will change their mind. You'll teach that readers take their interpretations through a process of drafting and revision.

Your hope is that these sessions encourage students to both *revise* their initial interpretations and to entertain alternate perspectives, possibly adapting their ideas to the ideas of others. This concept of a journey of thought is an important one in this curriculum. After all, consider how the bends in the road of a unit signal that the units, themselves, are designed to support journeys of thought.

Another way for interpretations to become broader and deeper is to attend to the minor characters that may play important roles in stories. To notice those who may be overlooked is a valuable strategy for understanding more complex texts. It is also an important step in becoming more critical readers. As students read increasingly complex texts, the story's minor characters and subplots will become increasingly important to understanding the story as a whole as well as how and why events unfold.

This is one of those times when Readers' Theater, even in a small way, can bring alive the voices of characters and help students to step into their shoes. In fact, you'll ask your students to do some improvisation to act out characters' roles. You might say, "Let's have you and your club mates pick a part in one of your books that seems to be written in bold. Each of you should take on one of the characters that has a role in that passage and talk to each other from within your character's perspective."

Across this bend, you will help children know that although, yes, reading is all about holding tight to the often hair-raising, death-defying dramas of historical fiction books, reading is not only about following the literal action of the story. Reading is also about coming away with deeper thoughts about what bravery or friendship is, about how loss or defeat can be handled, or what compassion feels like. This bend aims to help youngsters read between the lines so they come away with bigger ideas about their lives and their world.

Bend III: The Intersection of Historical Fiction and History

In the third bend, you'll begin by teaching students to deepen their understanding by turning to nonfiction, beginning with primary source images. By studying images from the time period they are reading about, children deepen their engagement with that period, building knowledge and adding to the details they have learned to recognize as historical to that era. They also notice new information and perspectives. They will take this knowledge back to their novels, looking for the places that where nonfiction intersects or adds to what they're reading about in their novels. This work will ignite energy in the room. Students will the love the opportunity to see pictures of real-life people and places from the time periods in their novels. Building on their reading interpretation work, you can teach students that the same guidelines apply to *any* interpretation—whether it be about a story, a photograph, a piece of nonfiction, or life in general. This work is important because it will extend children's understanding and also because it teaches them a lifelong habit. Whenever they read about unfamiliar places and times, they'll develop a deeper relationship with that setting if they study some of the primary sources of that place, especially images.

This lesson is closely followed by one in which students develop their own questions as they read, try to answer them, and generally learn more by turning to nonfiction sources. As children get older and tackle more texts on unfamiliar topics, learning to go outside the text for explanations will be crucial. Here, you turn children to on-the-run research, coaching them to study a bit, go back to their novel, figure out how what they've learned fits with or extends what they knew, and keep reading—and then do it all again! Children can also learn information from their historical narratives, of course.

You'll remind your students to bring all the strategies they've learned from their studies of biography and narrative nonfiction, to actively learning from historical stories.

Then, too, you'll ask students to keep in mind the important question, "Whose history am I learning about?" You'll guide them to read critically, remembering that historical fiction novels can provide powerful glimpses into *some* people's perspectives on a historical event, but it's not *everyone's* perspective. You'll also teach students to consider their stories through the lens of power, including thinking about who has power, how that power is visible, and where there are signs of resistance. Kids love this work, although interestingly, they seem to need your help in order to initiate it. As they do this work, especially as they learn about people's perspectives, you'll teach them to avoid assumptions and overgeneralizations. It's important, for instance, that when reading *Number the Stars*, children learn about the perspective of young Danish children during WWII. That's new learning for fourth-graders, and it's learning they can get only from stories. It's also important that they don't think the Rosens represent all Danish Jews, or that all young Danish girls had sisters who were in the Resistance.

As you bring the unit to a close, your emphasis will turn to a lot of cross-text work and critical literacies. After all, the work children did is not important only because it helped them engage with *Number the Stars* or *Bud, Not Buddy*, gorgeous as those books are. The work matters because it will also deepen their reading practices of any book. You'll set children, therefore, to comparing and contrasting themes across novels and to thinking about the implications of the lessons they've learned from their stories for the lives they live.

In the final session, you'll encourage your students to reflect on the work of the unit and acknowledging the personal nature of that work by asking, "What's important here? What's this really, really about—for me, for my life?" You might wrap up with a little keynote, calling on the great men and women who inspire us to live better lives. Then, you'll tell your students that you're going to gather all their beautiful work, and put it on display, so others in your school can see what it really looks like when people are different because of what they read.

At the culmination of this unit, your children should be powerful readers. We want, here, to do nothing less than to help you show children that reading matters because it teaches us how to live. Books give us insight into lives that we wouldn't otherwise understand. They illuminate issues of social justice, they make visible the dilemmas of history and of the everyday transactions of our lives. They should leave us with lasting lessons, deeper empathy, and mentor role models. At the end of the unit, therefore, you'll bring the lessons students have learned from their books to bear on the urgent social issues that shape their lives. You'll move your students to be affected—no, to be transformed—by their books, so that we may all try to live lives of greater courage and integrity.

ASSESSMENT

Throughout the year, your instruction has been informed by continual assessment, and this unit is no different. When the time comes to re-assess your students' reading levels, you'll use running records as one form of assessment. Most schools and districts have two to three set times across the year when they measure students' reading levels. That said, if you have students far below grade level, you'll want to assess them more often to make sure they are making progress (even if it is just a brief, informal assessment in which they read a bit of a book to you and talk about what they read). Then too, you'll want to make sure that you are giving students of all ranges and abilities an opportunity to read increasingly harder texts. Book clubs are a great way to introduce a student to a new level because the other club members act as a built-in support network. If one of your students appears to be tottering between, say, levels R and S, use this opportunity to push him or her into that level S text. You may start off by giving this student a book introduction, an introduction to the time period, or other scaffolds. For these students who are just now reading at a new level of text complexity, you'll want to be watching for how they handle increased complexity, density, and length. Be alert especially for signs of disengagement and engagement. Watch their reading logs for possible declines or inclines in volume of reading.

Because this is a spring unit, most of your readers should be able to handle books around levels R and S, though obviously you'll have a range of readers. Each club member will read more than one book, so they are studying historical fiction, not just "a book." For these book clubs, you'll need multiple copies (usually four) of a few historical fiction books within one era and at within-reach levels. Assess your library and your school's book room and budget to determine if this is doable. If not, tailor the plan to your situation. For example, if you do not have four copies of a few books for each club, do you have sufficient numbers of duplicates so that you can support children working in same-book partnerships, instead of clubs? If so, perhaps members of a partnership can read copies of the same book, progressing in sync through it, perhaps later swapping books with another partnership that might be reading books set in the same era (and perhaps in this way children will be able to sometimes talk as a foursome). Can children get to the library or order used books? Do some readers have Kindles they can upload ebooks on? The point is to be innovative and flexible, so you and your children will find ways to read in clubs.

It is crucial that kids feel some sense of ownership over the composition of these clubs—and that the clubs work well for several weeks! There are a few ways to help children have input and for you to manage these selections in order to move your readers forward. One is for children to write letters about the people with whom they might like to read and the reasons they think those readers would be a smart choice as study partners. Another is for you to study your children ahead of time, and entice them into clubs that you think will support and challenge them. When you pull a few children together and say, "I've been thinking about you as readers, and I think you might do some beautiful work together. Let me explain why . . . ," they'll be pleased with their club!

You'll probably want to form mostly leveled clubs, so that you can channel them occasionally as guided reading groups, or actively help students—both your strongest readers as well as your lower level readers—move up bands of text complexity. You may also have clubs of avid readers who will simply read more books than other clubs. And a few clubs don't have to be exactly leveled—kids can read together within a range, as long as that range is reasonable. The structure of some clubs, then, can provide readers with support for texts that are a notch harder than those they have been reading. This lets you engineer clubs so that some readers are working with books (and classmates) that are a bit of a stretch. You may also put a child who is an especially strong reader into a club of less-experienced readers, deciding that although this means that individuals will be working with texts that are a bit easy, the opportunity to step into a leadership role might help that individual grow, as might the nudge to read books more slowly.

The point is, not all clubs need to be formed with precisely the same logic, and it's easy to talk to children in such a way that they are honored that you thought about a club for and with them. Usually, children will feel as if they chose these clubs, or were honored to be asked to join one—but really, you'll

have been involved in those negotiations, often suggesting groups that you know will be effective.

You'll probably want each club (but not the whole class) to tackle a time period and issue in history (e.g., World War II and the Holocaust, the early 1900s and immigration to the United States, Westward expansion, civil rights, Ancient Greece, the Depression) because you'll have a wider range of choice and levels. This way, too, it's clear that students are studying the literary tradition, not the social studies content. Since clubs bring readers together around shared books, you'll need multiple copies of lots of books on the eras that your readers will convene around, with the books within each era roughly equivalent in difficulty. However, you'll need larger quantities of different titles if the books are easier because the children will read through more of them.

You will find that provisioning kids with books is a challenge. If children reading level K/L/M books are to maintain a strong volume of reading, they will need to read a small stack of K/L/M books each week throughout the unit. If the unit runs for a month and children are reading only from your collection of historical fiction, you'll need multiple copies of at least a dozen K/L/M books, all set in a single era! Readers of R/S/T books will read longer texts, so they'll get through them more slowly, but they'll still read *at least* three books during a five-week unit, as well as related picture books and nonfiction texts.

All this goes to say that most teachers need to figure out ways to provision students with the books for this unit. If you have a limited collection of books, you can decide that children will read books set in one historical era for two weeks and another (perhaps related) era for the second two or three weeks. For example, Sam, Aly, Josh, Fallon, and Isaac of the Freedom Fighters club will read a few books on civil rights and then shift to a couple of books on a different historical era. Alternatively, you might suggest that children read the multiple copies that you *do* have at a slow pace, discussing each little bit of those books with each other, and meanwhile maintain a voracious, independent reading life, reading single copies of historical fiction books and nonfiction titles related to the selected era.

A word about volume and rate: For some students, their club book will fulfill their independent reading life. That is, if a child is reading thirty to forty pages a day of historical fiction *and* jotting and thinking about that book, that might be all that child can do. For other children, their book club book won't fulfill their independent life. These kids will usually be avid readers or those who were moving up levels in a genre, such as graphic novels or realistic fiction. They will want to be reading another independent book at the same time, which may or may not be historical fiction. As you study your kids before the first session and get them into the right clubs, help them also figure out the books they need to fulfill their reading life.

So that's what children will read. Meanwhile, what will you read aloud, to anchor your instruction? We anchor the unit with Lois Lowry's narrative, *Number the Stars*. It's relatively short, it's beautiful, and it's important. Lowry writes with an attention to detail, a layering of symbolism, and a sense of respect for the multiple perspectives of the historical as well as fictional characters. Children will learn an enormous amount about what it was like to be a young child in Denmark during the German occupation. They'll also learn about courage, sacrifice, and growing up. Another gorgeous aspect of this book is that it is complicated without being difficult. That is, it will be accessible to all your students, especially when you bring it alive with your voice. And it will reward the analytical strategies you'll be teaching. We pair the novel with a picture book, *Rose Blanche*, which tells the story of a young German girl, growing up in the same years. It's also a story of courage and sacrifice, though sadly, she does not get a chance to grow up.

Both books have won awards, and we're sure you'll love them if you haven't read them yet with children. They are serious stories. They are war stories. Bad things happen in them, though the violence is mostly hinted at and off-the-page. And ultimately, both stories are about the triumph of love and courage over evil. Of course, you can choose different texts. One note: If you choose different read-alouds, keep in mind that you may need to change the order of some lessons, because these lessons are carefully sequenced so that the read-aloud will set children up to practice the particular strategy taught in the lesson. You can do similar sequencing, but it will take some forethought, so don't let it catch you by surprise.

One other quick note: As gorgeous as these books are, remember that the point is for children to get stronger at reading any novels—not just *Number the Stars*, not just *Bud, Not, Buddy*, not even just historical fiction. So as

you demonstrate and refer to your anchor texts, make every effort to also demonstrate that these reading strategies are transferable. You'll see, as you look ahead, that the language of the teaching points emphasizes this attitude.

ONLINE DIGITAL RESOURCES

A variety of resources to accompany this and the other Grade 4 Units of Study for Teaching Reading are available in the Online Resources, including charts and examples of student work shown throughout *Historical Fiction Clubs*, as well as links to other electronic resources. Offering daily support for your teaching, these materials will help you provide a structured learning environment that fosters independence and self-direction.

To access and download all the digital resources for the Grade 4 Units of Study for Teaching Reading:

1. Go to **www.heinemann.com** and click the link in the upper right to log in. (If you do not have an account yet, you will need to create one.)
2. **Enter the following registration code** in the box to register your product: RUOS_Gr4
3. Under **My Online Resources**, click the link for the **Grade 4 Reading Units of Study**.
4. The digital resources are available in the upper right; click a file name to download. (For any compressed ("ZIP") files, double-click the downloaded file to extract individual files to your hard drive.)

(You may keep copies of these resources on up to six of your own computers or devices. By downloading the files you acknowledge that they are for your individual or classroom use and that neither the resources nor the product code will be distributed or shared.)

If you use *Number the Stars* as your mentor text, follow the pacing guide to make sure you and your students are prepared for each session. Some minilessons will require you to read aloud text during the session, but to keep minilessons brief and maximize club and independent reading time, we suggest that you set aside an additional block of time for most of your read-alouds.

NUMBER THE STARS PACING GUIDE

Session	Read Aloud during the Minilesson (Refers to *Number the Stars*, unless otherwise noted)	Read Aloud before/after the Minilesson (Refers to *Number the Stars*, unless otherwise noted)
BEND I		
Session 1	*Rose Blanche* by Roberto Innocenti, or a similar historical fiction picture book	No specific reading
Session 2	Chapter 1, pp. 1–2 (up to "The corner was just ahead.")	The rest of Chapter 1 (*after* the minilesson)
Session 3	Revisit Chapters 1 and 2.	Chapter 2 (*before* the minilesson)
Session 4	Revisit Chapter 1, p. 2 and pp. 8–10.	No specific reading
BEND II		
Session 5	*The Tiger Rising*, Chapter 10, or another favorite read-aloud *Number the Stars*, Chapter 3, pp. 24–25	Chapter 3 (*before* the minilesson)
Session 6	Read aloud all of Chapter 5 (for the first time).	Chapter 4 (*before* the minilesson)
Session 7	Students should be able to discuss what they've read so far in *Number the Stars*.	Chapters 6 and 7 (*before* the minilesson)
Session 8	Chapter 6, pp. 50–53	Chapter 8 (*before* the minilesson)
Session 9	Chapter 9, pp. 74–81	Chapter 9 (*before* the minilesson)
Session 10	The poem "Things" by Eloise Greenfield	Chapters 10 and 11 (*before* the minilesson)
BEND III		
Session 11	Chapter 2, p. 12	Chapters 12 and 13 (*before* the minilesson)
Session 12	Chapter 15, p. 118	Chapters 14 and 15 (*before* the minilesson)
Session 14	Chapters 8–10, pp. 67–87 (Teaching) Chapter 16, pp. 123–24 (Active Engagement) Chapter 14, pp. 109–10 (Share)	Chapter 16 (*before* the minilesson)
Session 15	Students should be able to discuss what they've read so far in *Number the Stars*. Chapter 1, p. 5 Chapter 5, p. 47	Chapter 17 (*before* the minilesson) [End of *Number the Stars*]

ear Teachers,

You have reached what is likely to be one of your last units of the year. Congratulations. Take a moment or two to reflect on all the ways your students have already grown across this year and glory in that. Taking some time to glory in growth and to celebrate is important. You and your students have worked hard. Their efforts should be showing clearly.

By now you know how our suggestions for pre-unit work go. Our first piece of advice is to read the front matter of the book so that you can gain an orientation to the unit. Our second piece of advice is to give a performance assessment prior to the unit starting, which will help you to determine a baseline for where your students are and also get some ideas for where you want to take them during this unit. This assessment, as you remember, is designed to assess some of the skills that are most essential to this unit and across the standardized assessments many students take.

By now, you've likely got a sense of what helps to make the assessment go the best it can and you've figured out with your colleagues the ways that are best for you to give this assessment. Remember that these decisions need to be made and implemented in sync with what your colleagues are doing. And of course, whatever tips and ideas you have—we're all ears. Let us know what you've done and we'll funnel what we learn into the Online Resources and share it with other schools and districts so we can all get stronger at doing this work together.

So go forward again today, making the performance assessment work for you and your children. And do make sure to take some time to celebrate the journey.

Thanks,

Lucy and Mary

Reading Analytically at the Start of a Book

B Y THIS TIME IN YOUR YEAR, it is important that your teaching is lifting *your* energy, generating passion and purpose and energy that you pass on to your students. No approach to teaching will ever work if it doesn't tap an energy source in *you*—the teacher.

Before launching this unit, think of a favorite historical fiction book. Perhaps you read *Exodus*, Leon Uris's dramatic novel about the founding of Israel, imagining yourself living Kitty's romantic, dangerous life. Or perhaps you read *Witch of Blackbird Pond*, shivering at the frightening violence of the Puritans. Share with students how you were swept up by that story or some other historical fiction. More than that, if you have ever read a book with friends and come to see that book through new eyes because you read it with others, bring that experience to your students.

> *"You'll help your students grasp that setting is intimately related to atmosphere and mood, and to be alert to the emotional as well as the physical setting."*

In this session, you invite—even entice—your children into the world of historical fiction, and then you immerse them in figuring out, at the very beginning of their narratives, when and where the story is taking place and *what kind of* place it is. You'll often see that children are asked to do this work on the new reading exams, and the questions there are usually framed as analyzing a part of the text in relation to the whole. For example, children might be asked about why the author begins a story a certain way, and the answer will be to build tension, or to introduce the conflict, and so on. This work matters outside of and beyond state tests, though. When young readers begin a book or story, they often speed

IN THIS SESSION, you'll teach students that readers pay particular attention at the start of a book to analyze the setting—when the story takes place, where, and what this place feels like.

GETTING READY

✔ Review the "Getting Ready" section in An Orientation to the Unit, which contains helpful information about effective ways to organize clubs. Form clubs prior to today's session.

✔ Review the "Analyzing Parts of a Story in Relation to the Whole" strand of the Narrative Reading Learning Progression.

✔ Be ready to describe, retell, or read an especially dramatic part of a historical fiction novel that you've read (see Connection).

✔ Be prepared to give a picture book to each club. We suggest books set in the Holocaust and WWII, which is the read-aloud subject, or in the era each club is likely to study (see Link).

✔ Choose a historical fiction picture book or short story to read aloud during today's minilesson, such as *Rose Blanche* by Roberto Innocenti (see Teaching and Active Engagement).

✔ Introduce the unit anchor chart "Readers of Historical Fiction . . ." (see Link and Homework). 👆

✔ Prepare the charts "Creating a Constitution for Your Club" and "In a well-run club, members . . . ," which you will reveal during the share.

ahead, waiting for the plot to get to a big, exciting moment, not realizing that the author is doing some important work in this first part.

Today, as each student begins their new book, you explicitly call students' attention to the work an author is doing at the very beginning of that book. You'll then coach your students, as they continue to read, to notice when and how things are changing in their story. That act—of noticing that a new part is important—is the act of a knowledgeable and attentive reader, one who understands that authors insert scenes for a reason. The most common work that historical fiction authors do at the beginning of a story, for example, is to establish the details of the historical setting, including its tone—which is often one of impending conflict. You'll help your students grasp that setting is intimately related to atmosphere and mood, and to be alert to the emotional as well as the physical setting, realizing setting incorporates not just physical details but also how a place feels. The point of today's session, then, is not simply to entice children to be swept up by the settings in their historical fiction novels. It is to help students be attentive to the tone and atmosphere in a setting and more alert to growing tensions.

Reading Analytically at the Start of a Book

CONNECTION

Tell a story of how a historical fiction book swept you up and took you to another time and place. Bring that story to life, making your synopsis dramatic.

"Readers, last night as I was searching for something in our dusty attic, I saw, sitting on top of a box, an old paperback. I forgot about what I'd come for and picked up the book." I used my hands to simulate rippling the pages. "With its stained cover and wrinkled pages, it looked as if it had been read a hundred times. The cover showed a tanker ship, a rough-looking man with a machine gun, and beautiful woman in a nurse's uniform. The title, in large block letters, said, *EXODUS*."

I made my voice more urgent. "Readers, when I saw that title, I was back on the deck of a ship, with Kitty, an American nurse, and Ari, an Israeli soldier, and around us, a group of orphans who were starving themselves to death. It was 1946, a year after World War II ended. The children were refugees from the Holocaust, the death camps the Nazis built to exterminate the Jews. They had been taken from their families and hidden from soldiers and dogs in attics and basements. And now, finally, they were anchored off the shores of the Promised Land, the only place in the world where Jews could be safe. But the British wouldn't let them land. To convince them, the orphans had gone on a hunger strike.

"Readers, I first read this book when I was thirteen. It was my first experience with historical fiction—with stories that are set in other times and places. Until *Exodus*, I never knew that a book could take you to places where characters could be so brave, could sacrifice so much, could endure such danger and loss."

I sat up straighter and looked directly at the children, "Readers, when I left the attic, I almost forgot what I'd come for because I was thinking so hard about how to live a life of courage and commitment, like those children. *Exodus* made me want to make a life that added up, that was big and important."

Use your experience as a reader of historical fiction to talk up the genre and the unit in general.

"Readers, there is something so enthralling about stories set in the midst of historical events. The stories happen in war zones, in dust storms, in wild and wondrous places. The stories let you face threats that you'll never encounter in your lifetime."

You can, of course, substitute a different book you especially loved. Either way, as you talk about the book, pretend to be holding it— or really hold it—and feel its weight in your hands. Doing so lets the children imagine the book, too. It is convenient that Exodus *and* Number the Stars *are set in the same era, as the backdrop for* Exodus *helps to set children up for understanding* Number the Stars, *but that was actually just an accident.*

You'll notice the use of words such as courage *and* commitment, *and* exterminate *and* sacrifice. *This kind of language helps your children know that they are embarking on something exciting.*

✤ **Name the teaching point.**

"Today I want to teach you that at the very start of a story, readers pay particular attention to the mood and atmosphere of the places in which stories are set. Readers realize that the story will almost never say, 'This shows that trouble is brewing' or 'This shows a sense of hope,' so you must assemble clues to figure out what kind of place this is."

TEACHING

Set children up to look and listen to the start of a historical fiction picture book. Suggest that because you know the genre, you are alert to details of the setting, expecting trouble to brew.

"During your work with nonfiction, you noticed that nonfiction readers rev up their minds before embarking on reading. Readers build their expectations of what is to come before reading *any* text. Because historical fiction is always set in a time and place unlike your own, the work of getting ready to read historical fiction will require you to notice details about the setting. Here is a tip: trouble will be brewing. Be alert for signs that things are changing, and not in a good way. Look for how the author gives you clues at the very start."

"Let's look at this book, *Rose Blanche*." I show it, then say, "This story is about a girl who lives in a small town in Germany, during World War II. The author, Roberto Innocenti, said that he wanted to write a story about a place where something terrible is happening, that most people want to ignore." I looked ominously around the classroom.

I then showed the picture on the first page, and said, "Remember, we're asking, 'What clues is the author giving me that suggest what kind of place this is?' We're noticing details that suggest change or trouble." My finger moved on the page from one thing to another. Students took in the girl in a brown dress, standing in a crowded town square, holding a red flag with a swastika. Around her, others were doing the same, while soldiers climbed into trucks.

I read:

My name is Rose Blanche.

I live in a small town in Germany with narrow streets, old fountains, and tall houses with pigeons on the roofs.

One day the first truck arrived and many men left. They were dressed as soldiers.

Winter was beginning.

Now the trucks follow each other under the school windows. They are full of soldiers we don't know, but they wink at us.

They drive tanks that make sparks on the cobblestones. They are so noisy and smell like diesel oil. They hurt my ears and I have to hold my nose when they pass by.

This teaching point and most of the content of this unit pertains to complex texts. Reread the first pages of The Tiger Rising *with the lens of noticing the emotional atmosphere. You'll see that many of the details at the start of that story, too, create an emotional atmosphere.*

This is a picture book. It is common to launch a unit by reading aloud a short text. The use of a short text allows you to overview the work readers do at the start, the middle, and the end of a text, all within a day or two.

It would be pretty surprising to find historical fiction set in a place where nothing much is happening! The trick is to get children to notice how the authors are laying clues right from the start.

The illustrations in this book are done by the author, and so the pictures give extra support to readers. You'll want to show them as you read. You can read aloud just a tiny passage, as is typical in minilessons.

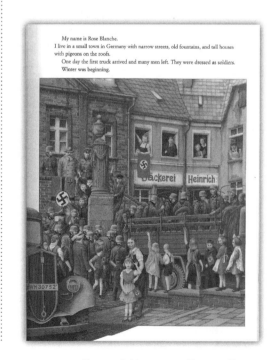

"What does this place look and feel like? Hmm, . . . it is a small town in Germany, with narrow streets, old fountains, tall houses with pigeons on the roofs. It sounds like it's been an old, quiet place—even a peaceful one." I looked back at the text and said, "But did you notice trouble brewing?"

Hands shot up, but I quelled them, shifting out of the reader's role to say, "I'm going to pay attention to the trouble that is brewing—so compare what you are thinking with what I do. See if you can get tips from how I do this." Then I shifted back into the reader's role and continued. "Hmm, . . . Rose Blanche says it's starting to be a place full of trucks and soldiers who wink, but still, they're soldiers. And they drive trucks, but they drive tanks, too. Instead of birds, it sounds like engines, and it smells like diesel.

"Do you get the idea that I get, that this is becoming part of a war?"

Restate the work you just did to analyze the setting, providing steps that the children can follow as they practice this work with other passages.

"Do you see how I did that? The most important thing is I *expected* the author to give clues at the start of the story. So I didn't just let the story fly by me, waiting for something big to happen. Instead, I was alert right from the start, looking for clues about the setting. I was especially alert to signs of trouble brewing—to clues the author gave about what this place feels like."

ACTIVE ENGAGEMENT

Read aloud the next section of the book and ask children to pay close attention to details about the setting, recording their ideas. Then ask them to share and reflect with a partner.

"Now it's your turn to try this. I'm going to read a bit more. Be alert to clues the author gives you that tell you what kind of place this is, and if trouble is brewing."

> Sometimes it seems things haven't really changed. But my mother wants me to be careful crossing the street between all the trucks. She says soldiers won't slow down.
>
> Lots of times I walk by the river, just looking at it. Branches float along and sometimes old, broken toys. I like the color of the river. It looks like the sky.
>
> The trucks are fun to watch. We stand in the doorway as they pass. We don't know where they're going. But we think they're going someplace on the other side of the river.
>
> One day one of them stopped so the soldiers could repair the engine. A little boy jumped from the back of the truck and tried to run away. But the mayor was standing there in the middle of the street.
>
> He grabbed the little boy by the collar and brought him back to the truck. Then he smiled at the soldiers without speaking. And they thanked him.
>
> The sky was gray.

As in many minilessons, you will be inviting kids to do the intellectual work you are doing, asking, "What's important about this part? Did you notice clues about trouble brewing?" You want them thinking about their answer to that question. And for now, you plan to demonstrate, hoping that kids will notice the difference between their observations of trouble and yours, and learn from that. Soon you'll pass the baton to them.

You'll notice that you repeat the details the author just presented. These explicit details often fly past readers. First, restate the details, and then begin to retell them as atmospheric, as if they create a mood.

You may be torn between encouraging students to jot and encouraging them to drop their pencils and listen with every fiber of their beings. Some students listen better while moving their pencils, and others do not. You'll have a sense, by now, for whether it pays off to ask them to write while you read, or whether too many of them miss the story when they are jotting. Probably different children will make different choices—they should know by now what's best for them as readers of a fresh text.

The soldiers climbed back into the truck; doors banged shut and it pulled away. It happened very fast.

"Readers, turn and tell your partner what you are thinking about this place—the signs of trouble, how it's changing—compare your thoughts."

They did this. I listened alertly so I could quote some of what they said.

Celebrate the depth and variety of children's responses, sharing some of their insights so that they all hear, again, what this kind of reading work sounds like.

"Can I have your attention, please? Sam noticed that Rose Blanche says the river is getting dirty and is full of broken toys. That made him think that the author wants him to know that this place is becoming grim. He wondered who those abandoned toys belong to.

"I heard others say it looks like the war is getting closer. What are the signs?"

Children piped in with details. With coaching, they cited words and phrases from the text: the streets are more crowded with soldiers, the "soldiers won't slow down" to let people cross the street, "a little boy jumped from the back of the truck and tried to run away," the mayor "grabbed the little boy by the collar," the soldiers stuff the little boy back into the truck, there is more barbed wire in the pictures.

Debrief, naming the work students have been doing in such a way that it is transferable to other texts, other days.

"Readers, I love how you've been alert to details that help you to answer, 'What kind of place is this?' You've described how this place *looks* and also how it *feels*. You've also paid attention to the author's specific words that give the mood of the place. That's what strong readers do."

LINK

Send children off to read aloud a historical fiction picture book in small groups (the book clubs-to-be), alternating between reading, stop-and-jots, and turn-and-talks.

"Readers, we'll do things a little differently today. Here's a stack of spectacular picture books. I'll hand out a book and call out the names of kids who will read that book. Your group will spend the whole workshop with this book. One member will read a few pages aloud, pausing when it feels like kids are bursting to talk, and then will say, 'Stop and jot.' Everyone will write. After a few minutes of silent writing (no talking), the reader will read aloud a few more pages and will again say, 'Stop and jot.'

Teachers, you can say a little more and use richer language than the children actually do, although try to give them a sense that the observations you share arose out of their conversations. Show that the place is becoming menacing, and in that way, increase tension around the story. Most importantly, by inserting the words, "the author . . ." you take details that students notice and reframe those as evidence of why a part of the text is significant. Often, children will analyze the details of a story, but they do it as if the story is true, and the details real, not as if they are demonstrations of the author's craft.

Some of your readers will benefit from sentence starters for reading and speaking analytically. They'll also benefit from a menu of possible answers to the question: Why did the author include this part? For them, you might create a chart that looks something like this:

The author probably included this part in order to . . .

Introduce the conflict

or

Develop a specific mood or feeling

or

Show things are changing

"At the end of that second jot, your group will talk about what you are thinking. I know you'll be thinking about the tone of the place and signs of trouble. I've started our anchor chart, 'Readers of Historical Fiction. . . .' After a few minutes of talking, another group member can read aloud, and so it will continue."

ANCHOR CHART

Readers of Historical Fiction . . .

- Read analytically, studying parts that clue them in to the facts, feelings, or setting

Laying the Groundwork for the Upcoming Unit

TODAY YOU HAVE A CHANCE to observe group dynamics and tweak small-group memberships, if needed. If any of the groups seem off, swap members now as they work with picture books. By day's end, these groupings will be formally named as clubs that will last for the unit.

As children work today, resist getting too involved. Your priority will be to set kids up for tomorrow's club work with historical fiction books. You may want to interrupt some of the picture book work to say, "Can I tell you a secret?" Explain that a cluster of children will actually become a long-lasting book club, and help that particular club become excited about reading a line of books linked to a particular era. Introduce those books.

Children will probably take to today's activity like bees to honey. You've invited them to assume the role of teacher—reading aloud, calling, "Stop and jot" and "Turn and talk." If a group finishes, urge students to reread, pointing out how much one sees when rereading. If you have time to lift the level of this work, encourage them to cite details from the text, and to think about the author's language choices.

If many clubs are reading picture books related to the era that you imagine students will later study, you will want to engage their interest in that era. Let them know you were sure they would be particularly interested in the era. Do a quick book talk about some of the books they may read. Introduce them to one or two fascinating historical events. Take time to recruit their enthusiasm for reading the text sets that you have in mind. Say things like, "May I show you a book that I thought would be perfect for your club and see if you like it?"

Be ready to talk up the books (and the era) that club members will study. For instance, I wanted to convince a club to read about the Westward Expansion. Our collection contained the Little House series, which would require some promotion, especially for some of the boys, so I drew on the way some boys had enjoyed the Box Car series. "What I love most about this time period and specifically about the Little House series, is that everyone is a survivor. In Westward Expansion books, people have decided to pack up their lives and travel through storms, famine, disease—praying that life will be better in the new place. You and I *love* survivor books—and the Little House books are about a brave pioneer family that tries to survive. In fact, I'm curious about the decisions you would have made during that time—I can't wait to hear about what you think was most dangerous then."

MID-WORKSHOP TEACHING
Readers Bring Everything They Know to Their Reading

"Readers, I want to applaud how you are talking about the work authors do at the beginning of a story, especially how they lay out clues that show what's specific and unusual about the place in your story. Some of you are also beginning to talk about what your story might be about—some of the possible themes. What's important is that you're not waiting for anyone to tell you the work you can do as a reader. You know a lot about what's worth paying attention to in a story, and you're bringing that expertise to your reading. Keep it up—bring everything you know to these stories."

Constructing Book Clubs to Do Important Work

Point out that the groups are actually their clubs. Channel club members to do some of the work of constructing a club: a name, a logo, a constitution. Jot notes on chart paper while students are talking.

"Can I stop you?" I said. "The work you've done in your small groups today has been important work. As you've no doubt realized, these groups will be your historical fiction book clubs. Club members might, therefore, spend these last few minutes discussing how to make your club be the best it can be.

"You've all been in book clubs before, and in other clubs—sports teams, summer camp groups. When the United States was formed, it was almost like a giant club—Thomas Jefferson, Ben Franklin, and others gathered in a room in Philadelphia to make plans for the new nation and they wrote a constitution. So here's what I suggest, as a way to gather your expertise about clubs. You might also want to write a constitution, a way of working together. Some of you have done this in earlier units."

I gathered and charted students' ideas as they talked, and then revealed the chart with a list of some of the questions a club might ask. After a minute, I interrupted, "I want to clarify the third item on the list. This means how your club decides how many pages to read before each meeting. Readers, will you plan out the chunks of text to read now, or will you decide each time your club meets?

"So, readers, today marks the start of a new unit and the start of your club. You're inventing some

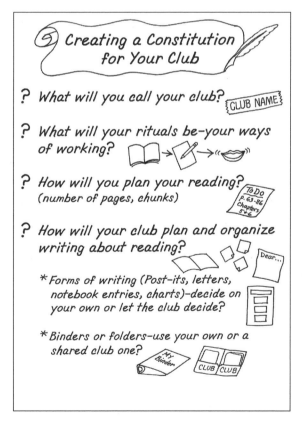

club rules and expectations. Before we end, be sure that you've gotten a club folder or binder, or some system for how you'll hold onto all your materials."

Before children departed, I let them know that tomorrow they would be reading in their club books and working with their club mates.

 ## PAY CLOSE ATTENTION TO THE SETTING OF A BOOK

Readers, tonight pay close attention to the work an author does to establish the setting at the start of a book. Choose whatever book you're reading, or a book you've read before and have on hand, and reread part of it, especially the beginning, using this lens. If you have picture books at home, you might try reading one of them. As you read, ask yourself the questions from today's anchor chart:

> **ANCHOR CHART**
>
> Readers of Historical Fiction . . .
>
> • Read analytically, studying parts that clue them in to the facts, feelings, or setting

Quickly jot your ideas about how the author establishes the setting, mood, and details that hint at possible trouble brewing.

As you did in class today, bring everything you know to doing this work well.

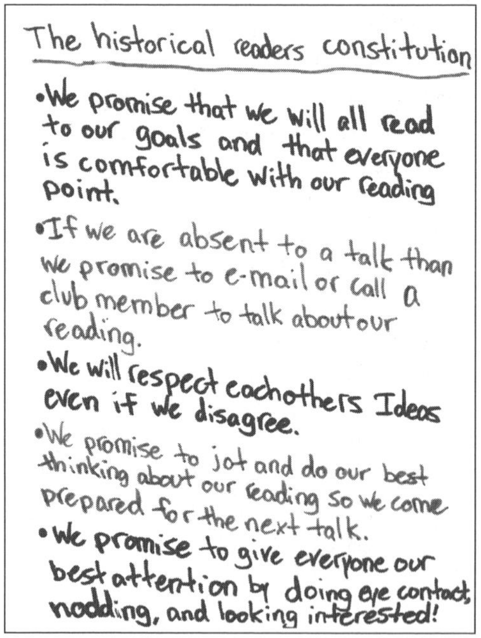

> The historical readers constitution
>
> • We promise that we will all read to our goals and that everyone is comfortable with our reading point.
> • If we are absent to a talk than we promise to e-mail or call a club member to talk about our reading.
> • We will respect eachothers Ideas even if we disagree.
> • We promise to jot and do our best thinking about our reading so we come prepared for the next talk.
> • We promise to give everyone our best attention by doing eye contact, nodding, and looking interested!

FIG. 1–1

Monitoring for Sense
Fitting the Pieces Together

TODAY YOU TELL CHILDREN that you've been in a historical fiction reading club with your colleagues. Frankly, if you do even a tiny bit of club reading with some colleagues, that will make a world of difference. Read even just the first few pages of the historical fiction book that your kids will be reading, then pause to name the work your mind was doing as you proceeded through those pages. Reach for accurate, precise words. You'll probably find you are trying to keep track of the pieces of the story and to fit things together—in short, to monitor for sense.

When we did this, we found that in the first chapters of a complex novel, there is so much new information coming at readers that it's important to gather the *who*, *what*, *where*, *when*, *why*. It was as if we were tacking these elements up onto a bulletin board. And we no sooner tacked elements onto the bulletin board than they began to morph. The little sister, at first unnamed, turns out to be Annemarie's younger sibling, Kirsti. Reading on, we learn that she and Annemarie have a bigger sister, too, around whom there is some mystery. Now a question gets added to the board: Why is the big sister introduced and then not mentioned again?

Other things were happening as we read. For example, as we passed our eyes over content-specific words such as *Copenhagen* or *Nazi occupation* or *the Resistance*, it was as if we'd pressed a link on our mental computer screen, and everything we knew related to those key words surfaced, forming background information.

This lesson sprang from that work. Today you'll teach students that strong readers begin a complex novel by actively working to piece all the bits of information together. Readers of complex novels know things will morph as they read on, so they construct a sense of the story as if in pencil.

IN THIS SESSION, you'll teach students that readers keep track of story elements as they read, continually building their understanding of what's going on.

GETTING READY

✔ If you are using *Number the Stars* as your class read-aloud text, we strongly urge you to follow our Pacing Guide, which you can find in An Orientation to the Unit.

✔ Review the strand "Monitoring for Sense" of the Reading Narrative Learning Progression.

✔ To channel students to sit with club mates, leave club markers around the meeting area, forming an informal seating chart (see Connection).

✔ Display a sheet of chart paper to act as your "mental bulletin board." Scrawl a few bits of information on the page to create a visual accompaniment to the minilesson (see Teaching).

✔ Display a portion of text from the suggested read-aloud text, *Number the Stars* (excerpt from pages 1–2), possibly on a document camera or Smart Board (see Active Engagement).

✔ Place maps and globes (or even iPads or laptops open to maps) near children's reading places so they may note the locations of their stories (see Active Engagement).

✔ Alert children that each club has a basket of historical era–based books at their tables (or other club locations) and each club member should take a book to read in class (see Link).

✔ Update Bend I anchor chart "Readers of Historical Fiction . . ." (see Link).

✔ Hand out copies of the anchor chart from Unit 1 *Interpreting Characters* "How to Build an Interpretation" (see Homework).

Monitoring for Sense
Fitting the Pieces Together

CONNECTION

Tell children that you and your colleagues have also formed historical fiction book clubs. Invite children to join you in researching the mind-work involved in this reading.

"Readers, when you gather, will you sit with other members of your clubs, looking for the club markers I've left in the meeting area? Plan to sit in the same spot throughout the unit."

Once readers had settled, I said, "Readers, the other fourth-grade teachers and I have formed a historical fiction book club, too. Yesterday, we sat alongside each other, reading. It was so quiet you could hear the pages turn. Later we compared notes on our thinking. I thought I'd tell you what *we* found ourselves doing and ask if today, *you* might each spy on yourself as you read and see if you do something similar."

Name the teaching point.

"Today I want to teach you that at the start of a complex text, readers often tack up important information they need to know on mental bulletin boards. Specifically, they make note of the *who*, *what*, *where*, *when*, and *why* of the book."

TEACHING

Tell children that when you began reading your historical fiction book, you took note of fast-flying information, filling in details as they emerged. Set children up to observe you doing this.

"I've realized that when starting a complicated novel, so much information comes at the reader so quickly that it's useful to catch the important stuff and pin it onto a mental bulletin board. The reader is trying to grasp the *who*, *what*, *where*, *when*, and *why* of the book. I meet a character and tack that one character up onto my mental bulletin board, and then I meet another and do the same, then I read on and find details about the first character, and those get added in, filled in.

"We're going to read one of the most gorgeous historical fiction books of all time: *Number the Stars* by Lois Lowry. This has been translated into a zillion languages, so we'll be joining a global community that is connected through this story."

◆ COACHING

The kids think of this unit as being about historical fiction, but you know its subtitle could be "tackling complexity." You are using this genre to teach kids how to handle more challenging narratives.

You may want to change the analogy to one that better suits your class. For example, instead of saying "mental bulletin board," you might say "the whiteboard in your brain" or "an imaginary Google Doc." It goes without saying that you can alter the examples in any minilesson so that it fits your context.

Always while you demonstrate, you hope that kids are doing the work alongside you. You set up that expectation through your language, inviting children to think along with you.

For now, I'm going to read just a bit and show you what I mean by tacking things up on a mental bulletin board. As I do this, you can do similar thinking and note-taking alongside me. In any case, after a bit it will be your turn to continue tacking stuff that you learn onto your mental bulletin board."

Chapter 1, Why Are You Running?

"I'll race you to the corner, Ellen!" Annemarie adjusted the thick leather pack on her back so that her schoolbooks balanced evenly. "Ready?" She looked at her best friend.

Ellen made a face. "No," she said, laughing. "You know I can't beat you—my legs aren't as long. Can't we just walk, like civilized people?" She was a stocky ten-year-old, unlike lanky Annemarie.

"So let's stop there." Turning to the board, I muttered to myself, "What am I mentally noting?" Then I added, by way of explanation to the kids, "Usually I wouldn't *record* what's in my mind, but for now, I'll make my thoughts visible." I jotted on the board:

Annemarie
- lanky
- best friends w/ Ellen
- eager runner

Ellen
- stocky
- best friends w/ Annemarie
- reluctant runner

Debrief in a way that names the strategies you used that others can use with other texts.

I paused and said to the children, "I record the main topic—a character's name, for example—and as I read on, I'll return to that name and jot new details as they emerge. It's sort of boxes-and-bullet notes."

ACTIVE ENGAGEMENT

Set children up to try the work you just demonstrated, taking notes about important information in the story.

"Let's continue on in the story. The information you learn in later parts of the text may need to be added alongside the notes from the start of it." I resumed reading:

She was a stocky ten-year old, unlike lanky Annemarie.

"We have to practice for the athletic meet on Friday—I know I'm going to win the girls' race this week. I was second last week, but I've been practicing every day. Come on, Ellen," Annemarie pleaded, eyeing the distance to the next corner of the Copenhagen street. "Please?"

Ellen hesitated, then nodded and shifted her own rucksack of books against her shoulders. "Oh, all right. Ready," she said.

"Go!" shouted Annemarie, and the two girls were off, racing along the residential sidewalk. Annemarie's silvery blond hair flew behind her, and Ellen's dark pigtails bounced against her shoulders.

Notice that you have tucked lots of little tips into your teaching. You should be able to reread any teaching section of any minilesson, noting a handful of precise tips. The reference to boxes and bullets will support work kids are doing in the writing workshop.

"Wait for me!" wailed little Kirsti, left behind, but the two older girls weren't listening.

Annemarie outdistanced her friend quickly, even though one of her shoes came untied as she sped along the street called Østerbrogade, past the small shops and cafes of her neighborhood in northeast Copenhagen. Laughing, she skirted an elderly lady in black who carried a shopping bag made of string. A young woman pushing a baby in a carriage moved aside to make way. The corner was just ahead.

I gestured for children to jot.

Before children had finished this work, I reconvened the class. "I'm noticing that you not only tacked up information about the characters, you also did this on places. When you read *Copenhagen*, many of you knew things about that city and added what you already knew to your notes, not just what you read! So smart!

Channel kids to compare notes with club mates. Clarify that comparing notes is not the same as merely sharing them.

Then I said, "I know you have more notes to jot, but will you and your club mates compare what you have already collected?" As children began talking, I circulated from one group to another. In many clubs, students were simply presenting what they'd noted in a round-robin fashion.

I intervened. "Readers, can I have your eyes?" Once I had children's attention, I said, "Let me remind you that I didn't say, 'Read what you wrote to each other.' Instead, I said, '*Compare* your notes.' How are your notes similar and different from your club mates' notes? Talk about this."

LINK

Send children off to read, asking them to jot important information in their reading notebooks to discuss with their club later and to read only up to the point in the text the club selects.

"So today, readers, you'll have about thirty minutes to read your club book, and then you'll meet with your club for ten minutes. Most of you are beginning a book. As you read, remember not only to read analytically, thinking "The author probably included this part in order to . . ." but also, make sure you are collecting and organizing key facts like who are the characters. What are their traits? What's changing in the setting? I added a point to our anchor chart as children went off to read.

ANCHOR CHART

Readers of Historical Fiction . . .

- Read analytically, studying parts that clue them in to the facts, feelings, or setting
- **Fit the pieces together: who, what, where, when, why, how**

As students work, you can decide whether to coach into their work or to do your own work at the front of the meeting area. If you decide to do your own work, you'll want to tack up the word Copenhagen *and beside it, in parentheses,* Denmark. *You will also want to add to your notes on the two characters, and tack up information about Kirsti, too.*

During read-aloud time later today or tomorrow you will continue reading aloud Number the Stars. You'll find the upcoming section (starting with the girls being accosted by soldiers on the street) is written in such a way that you'll not want to pause to tack up information on a mental bulletin board, but will instead read quickly, getting lost in the story. You might remind readers that the author gives readers signals for how to read a text. Sometimes the author signals that a section contains vital statistics for the reader to note. Sometimes, the story picks up its pace, as if the author is saying, "Put down your pencil and read. This is an exciting part!"

Fit the pieces together

Who? When? What? Where? Why? How?

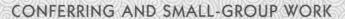

Responding to Predictable Problems as Children Read and Talk in Clubs

AS CHILDREN READ TODAY, draw on all you know about conferring into their reading from the earlier unit. Today's conferring section focuses especially on the specific challenges you'll encounter when you confer into clubs.

You'll feel like you need roller skates so you can move quickly among your students, making sure children are making smart reading plans. When children join clubs, sometimes reading itself gets lost in the excitement around group processes. Take a moment, then, to remind students to log their reading progress and be attentive to how much they are reading.

After children read for half an hour, you'll shift them into their clubs and then your conferring and small-group work will support conversations rather than actual reading. Before settling down to confer with one club, check in with them all to make sure they are generally on track. Fine-tune later.

Use your knowledge of bands of text difficulty to set clubs up to do some new work.

You will want to prepare readers not only for the challenges of the new book but also for the band of difficulty in which they will be working. If you can take a few minutes to read about bands of text difficulty in *A Guide to the Reading Workshop, Intermediate Grades*, this will allow you to introduce even a book that you don't know. You'll know the band of text difficulty to which the book belongs and you can say, "In the books you'll be reading a lot, you'll find . . ." and then you can set readers up for the challenges they're apt to encounter in that band. For example, you might say, "When reading books that are this complicated, sometimes a character says one thing—'I'm fine'—but the reader sees the character is acting and knows the character is *not* fine." You can coach a reader to anticipate that this might begin happening in their books.

To set one partnership up for their work with a band of text difficulty, for instance, I said, "Heads up. The books you'll be reading ask a lot more of you than the books you used to read. Before, someone would come right out and tell you what the characters were like. Like, when you read easier books, after you learned there had been a long, hard drought, with no rain, the main character said how he felt. 'It is hopeless,' a character might have said. 'There is nothing to buy. I saw children begging.' In those easier books, it wasn't hard to figure out what was going on or how the characters felt. But in the books you will be starting to read now, no one will come right out and tell you that a character feels hopeless (or whatever else the character feels). It will be like in life. A friend might be mad at you, but isn't saying anything directly, so you need to notice signs and put them together like a detective."

MID-WORKSHOP TEACHING **Preparing for Clubs by Rereading and Attending to the Things that Pay Off**

"Readers," I said, "in a few minutes, you'll have a chance to meet with your club mates. Before you talk with them, take a few minutes to review the part of the book you have read so far, thinking, 'Have I collected details, facts, about the characters and places that matter?' At the start of a story, you know to pay attention to the character's traits and to think, 'What drives this character?'

"Also, yesterday, when you read those picture books, you paid attention to the tone, the mood of the setting, thinking, 'What sort of place is this?' and 'Is trouble brewing?' Chances are good too much information was coming at you as you read today for you to pay attention to that—so reread, and notice that stuff now." I gave children a few minutes to reread, then channeled them to meet in their book clubs.

Help readers tackle predictable problems: Can club mates hear?

The most important thing that happens in a club is that people listen to each other. Clubs work when people lean in to really hear, listen hard, ask follow-up questions, and respond to what each member has to say. Start by checking the obvious. Can kids hear each other? Double-check that the way kids are sitting makes sense. Should they be around a smaller table or should they sit on the floor? Should one club sit in the hallway (usually a motivated, high-performing club that will work well without constant supervision)? Listen to the voices they use as well. Remember you needn't be the only one to coach children to speak up so they can be heard. If a child is mumbling, whisper to a listener, "Can you hear?" If the child says no, then say, "What are you going to do to address this?" Resist being the problem solver and empower children to take initiative.

Can club mates make efficient decisions?

Clubs require children to work collaboratively, meaning they need to learn to compromise, share power, and negotiate. In some classrooms, children have not had many opportunities to work in these ways, and their inability can derail the reading workshop for a bit. Although it might be tempting to give up on a particular class of children learning to collaborate, saying, "I still need them to learn to read, even if they are beastly to each other," it is a sad day if you give up on young people learning to get along.

Your kids have been in clubs before, so try to coach the club members to find ways to solve their own problems, but to do so efficiently. Time limits help. If club members struggle to negotiate over how many pages to read or who talks first, be clear that the decision needs to be made in minutes not days of time. Don't allow procedural talk to consume most of club meeting time.

What to do when kids dominate the club conversations.

You can be sure that even on this first day of club meetings, one or two children will dominate the club conversations. I would refrain from repeatedly admonishing the more dominant children to say less. Your talkative children are often readers whose minds brim with ideas, and you will want them to function as mentors and spark plugs within the group.

To manage this situation, work with the dominant child quietly, outside the club, perhaps saying, "You have the ability to talk well in a club, so I'm going to ask you to take on some of the most challenging roles. It is easiest to talk first, and harder to listen to the people who talk early on in a conversation, and then to build on their remarks. Could you try to get others to talk first and then, after their ideas are on the table, could you use your skills to build on one of the points someone else has made?"

You might suggest a club (or the class as a whole) take on the project of bringing out the quieter voices. Sometimes when a quieter speaker has something he or she wants to say, that child makes gestures that signal he or she is trying to get into the conversation. The quiet member might climb up on his or her knees, or begin to raise a hand and then back down. It is helpful if an attuned club mate notices these signs and says, "Did you want to add on?"

Similarly, once that child has said something, it is helpful if the next speaker doesn't jump in too fast on the heels of the quieter child, cutting that child short. Often after one quiet child speaks, if there is a little pool of silence, a second quiet child will speak into that silence, because it is easier to contribute when proceeding in the wake of a quiet child's comment. In the beginning, you might also consider having quick conferences or small groups with less secure readers, helping them to get ready to share ideas when club time comes along.

Listening to Others "Like Gold"

Ask your students to look around the room and notice how others are participating in club work, and then encourage them to look and act like engaged, caring readers.

After children talked in their clubs for five minutes, I said, "Will everyone freeze exactly where you are? Don't move your bodies! I want people to see how you are sitting or standing or leaning. Just turn your heads a tiny bit, so you can look around the room and notice who seems to be sitting in a listening way, regarding what club mates are saying as if it's gold. And who seems—from posture alone—to be disregarding other people's ideas?

"In this unit, you will be tackling complex texts and doing more sophisticated thinking. To do that well, you'll need to make a commitment to taking care of your club, which involves really listening to *every* member of your club. Talk briefly about what that kind of active listening looks and sounds like."

I listened in, and celebrated what they said. Then at the end of class, I notified students that tomorrow, they would be reading their club books and discussing them with their club mates.

Charts and small teaching tools act as reminders of your teaching.

CHOOSE A SELF-ASSIGNMENT FOR YOUR READING AND THINKING WORK

Readers, before you read tonight, think about this question: What work do you want to do in your mind as you read? You could read, collecting information about the people and the place. Or you could focus on the place especially. If you decide to do this, try to sense the tone of it, to note the details, to think about whether trouble is brewing. Notice how the setting seems to affect the characters—and know that it might affect different characters differently!

But you could also remember the work you learned to do during our last fiction unit, and draw on any of the work on the "How to Build an Interpretation" anchor chart from that unit, which is copied for you here. If you start developing ideas and interpretations now, the level of your book club conversations is sure to skyrocket.

◆ A DAY FOR ASSESSMENT ◆

Dear Teachers,

Today will feel familiar to you and to your students. By now you've seen the power that comes from students having the opportunity to get feedback on their work and to form goals and action plans that can carry their work to new heights. You've seen the energy and the resolve. And so have your students.

As you've done in previous units, we suggest that today you set aside time to engage students as active agents of their own reading development. By studying the rubrics and learning progressions next to your assessments of their work, by considering the logic behind your scoring, students can understand what the expectations are for their work. And, they can determine what their goals and action plans are for the future. Remember that one of your greatest jobs as a teacher is to help students to know where they are now, where they need to go, and how to get there. The goals should be transparent for students so they have a crystal-clear sense for what to do next. There is an enormous feeling of empowerment when you are in charge of your own learning. You feel ownership and determination, a readiness to do whatever it takes to improve. Remember that the goals for students should feel worthy—not completely out of reach but offering work that likely cannot be mastered in the span of one workshop. You'll want to support students in creating worthy goals for themselves as well as the action plans that will help them to reach those goals. What is most important is that as students move forward, they can ask themselves, "What is going well for me? And how can I push myself to do more to meet my goals?" It's this constant questioning, a constant seeking to be stronger, an embracing of mistakes as a chance to learn and to do more that leads to the mind-set of growth and of being a lifelong learner. It's how a person goes from good to great at anything.

Remember at the start of the first unit, we described the story of Lucy who crept through the wardrobe into Narnia and found herself on a great adventure. You'll no doubt recall that our heroine in the story made many decisions and was in charge of her own journey. Today is all about making sure that students know they are in charge of their own learning journeys, not just on this one day, but for their whole lives, that they are the hero/heroine of their own great learning adventure, and that it's up to them to shape that adventure.

Remember that the Online Resources will be a resource to you. There you'll find a more detailed description of how today's important work might go, as well as relevant rubrics, learning progressions, and exemplars.

To lifelong adventures in learning!

Thanks,

Lucy and Mary

Thinking across Timelines

Fitting History and Characters Together

DURING SESSION 1, you assessed children's current skill levels and hopefully gave them the opportunity to raise the level of their own work using the learning progressions. Most of that work focused on interpretation and analysis, and it may be tempting for you to bypass literal comprehension skills and dive into higher-level thinking skills. But here's the thing—as the books get more complicated, your students need help with the essential work of comprehension. The work of constructing a coherent storyline becomes challenging as stories begin to have multiple plotlines, backstories, characters who are not what they seem, and problems that remain unsolved. What we have found is that if you rush students to talk about theme and symbols without first working on basic comprehension, you risk students becoming fancy talkers whose ideas emerge from the glossy surface of the story.

This session and indeed this book aim to help kids attend to the details that give a story complexity. Specifically, this session will help them understand that in challenging novels, the passage of time becomes more complicated. Often events that are significant to the story happen before the story starts. For example, in the first chapter of *Number the Stars*, readers learn about prior events in history: German soldiers have already been in Copenhagen for three years, goods (including coffee) have been restricted during that time, brave Danish resisters exploded factories that could have become suppliers for the Nazis. There are prior events in Annemarie's family life too, including the death of the sister just before her wedding day. Information about that event and others will keep emerging across many pages of the book. Keeping the chronology of a story straight is especially challenging in complex texts because jumps in time are often not well marked.

Today you will zoom in on a particular challenge related to the complexity of time. You'll help readers think not only about the sequence of events in characters' lives but also the sequence of events in the historical setting. Events in the setting create chains of action and reaction that form the bedrock of any story's plotline. Specifically, you will let students know that in historical fiction, stories unfold along two timelines, not one. Readers must be aware of both timelines—the timeline of historical events and the timeline of the

IN THIS SESSION, you'll teach students that readers keep track of the ways in which characters' timelines fit with the historical timelines, deepening understanding of both characters and historical events.

GETTING READY

✔ Just prior to teaching today's minilesson, finish reading aloud Chapter 2 of *Number the Stars*.

✔ Be prepared to show a personal timeline of your life, showing how it is intertwined with historical events from the time in which you have lived (see Teaching).

✔ Make two wall-sized timelines—one historical and one character-based—to represent events in *Number the Stars*, making sure to leave large omissions. Have three large Post-its, labeled with missing points on the timelines, ready for students to work with (see Active Engagement).

✔ Make sure students have their book club books and materials (see Link, Conferring and Small-Group Work, Mid-Workshop Teaching, and Share).

✔ Add to the Bend I anchor chart "Readers of Historical Fiction . . ." (see Share).

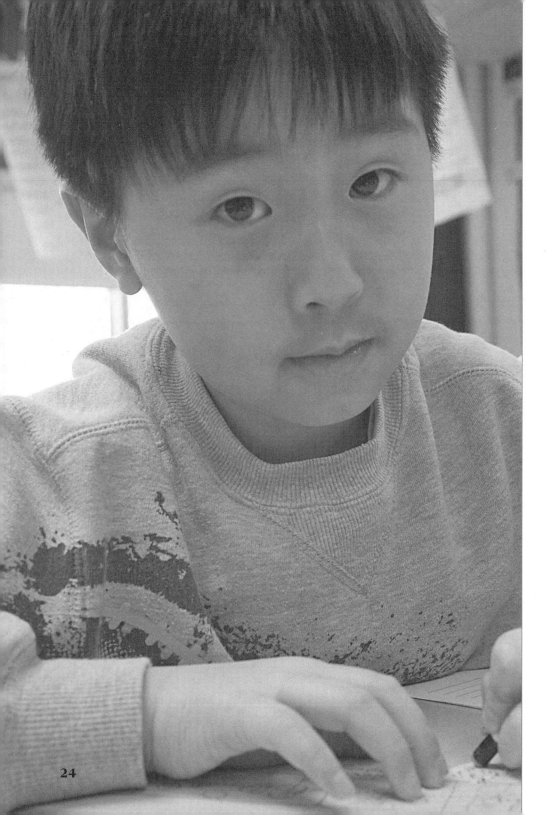

protagonist's life—and then must examine the relationships *between* those timelines. Readers should be thinking, "How does history influence the big events in the protagonist's life?"

For now, you'll encourage club members to make a timeline of historical events in their era on paper, although readers often do this in their mind's eye as they read. Because club members will read a bunch of texts about a historical period, they will soon see that each of their texts can be set alongside their emerging timeline of that era, with one text fitting alongside another.

"Events in the setting create chains of action and reaction that form the bedrock of any story's plotline."

In historical fiction, the answer to the question "Is the protagonist influenced by events in history?" will be "yes." Sometimes the historical events make themselves felt right away, as in *Number the Stars* and *Rose Blanche*. Other times, the historical pressures emerge gradually, seeping into the characters' and the reader's consciousness, as with *The Watsons Go to Birmingham–1963*. You will want your students to realize that the mix of time and place provides far more than a backdrop. The historical timeline affects the personal timeline of each character. Help students imagine the two timelines as woven threads.

Thinking across Timelines
Fitting History and Characters Together

CONNECTION

Tell children about how people you know responded to a big event in history, illustrating the way historical events initiate many cause-and-effect sequences.

"Readers, I recently finished Malala's incredible book about how she stood up to the Taliban so girls could get an education in Pakistan. She wrote how, after September 11th, the Taliban became a stronger presence in her village, shutting down more and more girls' schools, so that girls had no opportunity to go to school.

"That book got me thinking about all the people whose lives have been changed forever by historical events—like that one day on September 11th, 2001. The people who found themselves in wars. The children whose lives were changed. This amazing girl, Malala, who survived being shot by the Taliban, is now a world spokesperson for peace and education, winning the Nobel Peace Prize at age seventeen."

Extrapolate a larger message. History is comprised of many big things, each altering the course of people's lives, creating small personal stories.

"History is made up of big things that happen to a society, to a country, to the world. As historical fiction readers, you will become even more aware that the wars, revolutions, and discoveries you read about in textbooks actually *happened* as part of ordinary people's lives. There's the official history of the big events." I made a sweeping gesture. "Then there are the small personal stories of the people who had to struggle through them." I used my hands to show little ripples wafting out from the big events.

♣ **Name the teaching point.**

"Today I want to teach you that in historical fiction, there can be more than one timeline. There is the main character's timeline; there is also a historical timeline—and the two are entwined. To understand anyone, it helps to know the way that person's timeline intersects with the timeline of world events."

◆ COACHING

Many children—indeed, many adults—view history as something that has no relevance outside of textbooks. You will make your point that events in the world affect people's own personal timelines. You might use the story of September 11th and Malala, as I did, or choose another historical event that is relevant to your students' lives. You'll want to avoid having to do a lot of explaining, so choose something that affects your kids or an issue about which they have studied.

TEACHING

Retell your personal timeline, and a parallel historical timeline, to provide a real-life example of how an individual's choices (yours) are affected by historical context.

"I could make a personal timeline of part of my life. It might look like this":

- 1960: Moved to a farm in western New York.
- 1961: Started middle school. A man named Don Graves was my minister.
- 1961–1965: Taunted at middle school. Began tutoring kids in reading.
- 1965–1969: High school (tutoring)

"But here is my point. To understand the story of my life, or of any person's personal timeline, it is helpful to think about that timeline *alongside* a historical timeline of world events so it is clear how my timeline helps me organize events in my life—and how they fit against a backdrop of historical events as well. Let me tell you about my life, and you will see that my life is actually two intertwined timelines: a personal one and a historical one." I laid out a historical timeline alongside the personal one. "When I tell about my personal timeline, will you point to it (on the left); when I tell about the historical timeline, point to it (on the right).

Personal	Historical
1951: Born in Boston, Massachusetts	1951: Color TV introduced in U.S.
	Sputnik
	Berlin Wall erected.
	1953: Hydrogen bomb detonated by USSR.
1960: Moved to a farm in western New York. My parents built a bomb shelter in the basement.	1960: Beatles formed.
1961: Teased in middle school. Don Graves was my minister.	1961: JFK inaugurated. Peace Corps. Camelot.
Began tutoring reading in urban Lackawanna	1963: March on Washington
	JFK assassinated.
	Tension between U.S. and USSR
	1964: Gulf of Tonkin–Vietnam War
1965–1969: High school (tutoring)	1968: Dr. Martin Luther King Jr. assassinated.
	My Lai Massacre
	1969: Neil Armstrong walks on the moon.

Children have a hard time thinking about history with any sense of relativity. Hundreds of years can get lumped together into just the olden days. As the unit progresses, think about constructing a timeline of the historical events in the books the class has read. Imagine that on such a timeline, near the dot signifying World War I, children hang the book jacket for Letters from Rifka, *an immigration story about a Jewish family seeking refuge in America in 1919. Alongside the dot for WWII, the cover to* Number the Stars *will hang. The anti-Semitism in* Letters from Rifka *takes on greater significance because that story occurred twenty years before* Number the Stars, *which tells of Jewish families being rounded up and deported. You might even consider adding a few pictures of events from the town or city in which your children live, or a marker for the years they were born (or even the year you were born!), helping them to see that history is not just something that happens to other people, in other places. It will also be incredibly helpful to have a world map hung prominently in the classroom so that students can easily reference the cities and countries they are reading about.*

We encourage you to prepare your own timelines—you'll love doing so and the kids will be thrilled to learn more about you! If you don't want to try to do this, you could say, "Let me tell you about a friend of mine's timeline," and use mine.

I began, pointing to the historical timeline as I spoke. "During my middle school years, our country was practically at a war with what was then called the USSR and is now Russia." I then pointed to the left, briefly, as I said, "My family had a cement bomb shelter in our basement, in case war started.

I stopped pointing, letting the children do so instead. "Then the USSR detonated a huge fifty-megaton hydrogen bomb.

"In school we had practice air raids during which we'd line up against the wall with our arms up over our heads. It wasn't just the world that was scary for me—school was too. Like Rob in *The Tiger Rising*, I was preyed upon by kids with more power. I used to go to our basement bomb shelter sometimes to cry because it was private there." I scanned the room, noting that some students were signaling toward my personal timeline.

"The United States became involved in a war in Vietnam. There were peace protests, and civil rights activists like Dr. Martin Luther King Jr. spoke out for peace (right). John F. Kennedy, who'd become President, established the Peace Corps and talked about service: 'Ask not what your country can do for you; ask what you can do for your country' (right). The Beatles sang songs of peace and love (right).

"At that time, I was involved in peace work at our church. Mostly, I started tutoring people in reading in a settlement house."

Reveal an important turning point in history—and in your own life.

"Then on November 22, 1963, I upset my teacher in homemaking class by sewing an entire seam on a shirt backward. I probably wouldn't even remember such a seemingly small moment in my life, except for what happened next. Right after that, I saw teachers huddled in the hallway of the school, weeping. 'What happened?' I asked. 'He's dead,' they all said. President Kennedy had been shot.

"I remembered Kennedy's famous words, 'Ask not what your country can do for you; ask what you can do for your country.' I decided that the work I was doing, tutoring in reading, was important to me. What was happening in history was a big part of my decision to be a teacher."

ACTIVE ENGAGEMENT

Channel partners to try to fit new bits of information into existing timelines—including moments of backstory that happened before the story started.

"I started making timelines for our book, but haven't had a chance to finish them, so I'm hoping you can help," I said, revealing the start to two timelines—one personal, one historical.

Constructing the two timelines and their coherent story was not easy to do because a million historical events occurred during that time, and only some felt consequential to this very brief personal timeline. I wanted to show how the moments on both timelines link together in a somewhat cause-and-effect, integrated way. You'll find building your own timeline is fascinating. It will shed an intriguing light on your own life.

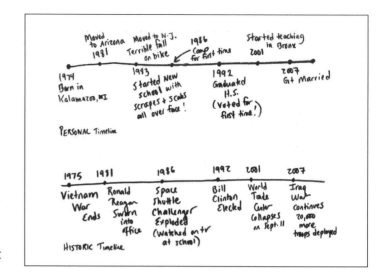

Annemarie's Timeline

- ?
- ?
- 1943: Annemarie is stopped by a German soldier while running down Østerbrogade Street with her best friend, Ellen. Her five-year-old sister Kirsti is with them.
- ?

Historical Timeline

- ?
- 1942: Hitler recalls the German ambassador from Denmark
- 1943: Jewish people living in Denmark begin to be rounded up for concentration camps
- ?

Then I showed three large Post-its with information on them and said, "I haven't yet figured out where these events go on our timelines."

- ◆ Papa tells Annemarie a story about King Christian riding his horse through the city

- ◆ Annemarie's older sister, Lise, is killed

- ◆ Denmark is invaded by Germany in 1940

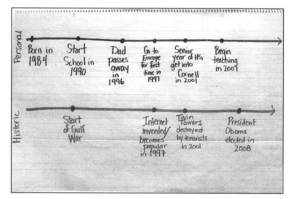

FIG. 3–1 Here you see two different teachers (born a lot later than us!) setting their own character timelines against a backdrop of history.

"Readers, as you read books that are more and more complex, you'll find that the author doesn't always help you make sense of which events happen in what order. *You* have to do that. And lots of times the author slips in events that may have happened long before the story even started! So that's where timelines can be so helpful. They help you create a sense of sequence, and that way you can think about how things might be connected, and about whether one event causes another. So right now, will you work with a partner, and try fitting these events into these two timelines?"

As students worked, I assessed their ordering of events, offering support when they were thrown off by jumps in time. Lots of children were unclear whether Lise died before or after Annemarie told Kirsti the story of King Christian because the storytelling came first in the book, the death of the sister, after. I coached some club members to talk between their two timelines, asking, "How did the events on one affect events on the other?" We put the Post-its into place on the timelines.

After students had worked for a moment, I said, "Readers, take a moment to talk with your club about the challenging parts of this work."

One student pointed out that sometimes things happened before the story started, like Lise's "accident." I smiled, knowing that later the students would have to reconsider Lise's death again, and revise their understanding of that event.

Debrief by popping out the transferable point.

"Readers, I want to stress that when you read historical fiction and, really, any complicated stories, not only do you need to keep track of jumps in time, you actually need to construct *multiple* timelines, to keep track of multiple events, and ultimately to *think between those timelines*."

LINK

Channel children to add working with timelines to their repertoire as readers. Prompt them to create timelines of their book club book across their fingers before returning to their seats.

"Readers, I invite you, right now, to try this work in your books: use the fingers of your left hand as the timeline of a main character and the fingers on your right hand as a timeline of historical events. I'm going to give you just a minute to do this quickly with someone who knows your book."

Long before the children finished their conversations, I interrupted. "Readers, sometimes your book does not explicitly tell you even one single historical event. It'll reveal the era when the story took place, but sometimes you won't find the historical events without learning more about those times. When that happens, you can still think about personal timelines, and eventually, you can read nonfiction material to learn about the historical timeline.

"It is time to get started on your reading. Decide quickly on your goalpost page and get started."

This minilesson teaches readers to keep several timelines unfurling as they read—a skill that is crucial when reading historical fiction and important when reading any complex fiction. In books that are level R and beyond, readers are expected to learn vicariously as they read, to come to know unfamiliar places and themes by reading about their relevance in characters' lives; hence the emphasis on creating two simultaneous timelines is an important one.

Your students will probably want to talk about this for longer than you have the time to give them. Treat this as "priming the pump" to get them ready to do more of this work as they read.

Rally Club Members around a Shared Goal

YOU WILL WANT TO CONFER and lead small groups to support students' independent reading of club books, as well as their club conversations. Book clubs offer you a perfect opportunity to provide differentiated small-group instruction. Use your knowledge of individual readers and of club book text levels and your learning progressions to fashion possible reading goals for your different clubs. Then meet with clubs to discuss their goals, sharing the evidence that you drew upon to derive possible goals and asking for input. For example, you might show members of one club that their Post-its and notebook entries suggest they grow ideas only about the main character, rarely attending to minor characters. You might then suggest entire members of that club might aim to notice ways in which minor characters impact the main character and the setting.

Encourage clubs to tackle goals.

When I approached the Civil War club, for example, I knew its members had read two picture books: *The Patchwork Quilt* and *Sweet Clara and the Freedom Quilt*. They were now inching through another picture book, *Nettie's Trip South*. Cutting to the chase, I said, "Readers, I notice you have slowed way down in your reading. Are the new words causing you trouble, or is something else getting in the way?" After some discussion, Gabe came up with the idea of using a stopwatch to time their reading and talking, as runners do. Although not my first choice as the most ideal solution, because I know few things matter more than that people have a sense of agency, I got behind his plan.

The Pioneers didn't need my help coming up with a goal—they announced that they aimed to bring books to life. They were less clear about ways to do this, so I told them about a club I'd worked with earlier. As a result, they decided to listen to an audio version of *Sarah, Plain and Tall*, paying close attention to how the actors said the book's words, and then to do their own reading aloud, trying to bring that same level of drama into it. Later, in the share, when clubs were meeting, I circled back, and saw Jasmine rise to her feet and read with a flourish a part of the text where Sarah shoos and plays with cows.

Pausing, Jasmine said, "That proves our point. Sarah will stay with the family because she is learning how to have fun. Caleb wouldn't have made that water go in her face if she wasn't part of the family. And Malik made a good point, about how Sarah's letter to her brother said *our* dune, not *their* dune."

I was glad the club was alternating between reading aloud and interpreting the text, and left them as they started discussing whether Sarah would still be lonely, deep down, if she did stay on the prairie.

When I met with the Freedom Fighters, I checked whether they could handle *Roll of Thunder, Hear My Cry*, as it is a long book. The club members explained that each had kept some notes of the *who*, *when*, *where*, and *why* of the story, and two of them were keeping timelines to track events. All that sounded good, but as they launched into conversation, it became clear that they were doing this work indiscriminately,

---

MID-WORKSHOP TEACHING
Readers Notice Dates in Their Books

"Readers, all eyes up here." I waited. "I want you to imagine this wall is a giant timeline. This corner is 1492 (I lilted, "In 1492, Columbus sailed the ocean blue"). Over here—in the far corner—is today's date. Will you make two Post-its that represent dates in your club's novel—guessing at them if you need to do so—and draw a map of the class to show where those Post-its would go in this giant timeline? Don't talk to your club or compare notes." I gave them a minute to do that. "Okay, back to work. You can read on, and later, in your clubs you can compare your ideas about the timeline in your book."

tacking up so many facts and events—major and minor—that there was no sense of significance. I coached them to be more selective of the events they put on their book's timeline. I suggested they might individually pick which events they considered most important in a chapter, and then tomorrow, as a club, they could discuss together why they made those choices, with the aim of settling on one or two most important events to timeline from most of the chapters.

My plan was that eventually I'd remind them to think about how events affected each of several main characters differently. They might ask, "How does Cassie react to this?" or, if she wasn't present in the scene, "Knowing Cassie, how *would* she have reacted to this situation?"

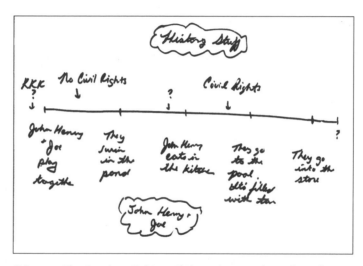

FIG. 3–2   The Freedom Fighters Club made a timeline of *Freedom Summer*.

Constructing a Class Timeline

Guide clubs to make sense of time in their novels, by building a quick class timeline of their stories.

"Club members, you can meet now, and I know you'll want to begin by figuring out where, along the timeline of our classroom wall, your story occurs. I've posted some dates. Will you put a big sheet of paper up on the wall to signal the start of your story? Then work together to construct two Post-it timelines on your table—one showing the personal timeline of your main character, and one showing the timeline of historical events in your novel. Just include the events that you think are most important to your character."

"Once you figure out the two timelines, begin talking about how the events that occurred in the setting influenced your character—or other characters. We'll talk more about that tomorrow." As children began to talk, I added a point to the anchor chart.

ANCHOR CHART

Readers of Historical Fiction . . .

- Read analytically, studying parts that clue them in to the facts, feelings of setting
- Fit the pieces together: *who, what, where, when, why, how*
- **Figure out the main character's timeline, and the historical timeline**

Figure out the main character's timeline, and the historical timeline

Character Timeline

Historical Timeline

WRITING ABOUT READING: EVENTS ON TWO TIMELINES

For homework tonight, in addition to reading, will each member of your club take on a character other than the main character, and will you add that minor character to your timeline, or create a timeline for that minor character, as best you can? Then will you take an important moment in the story and jot how your minor character responded differently than the main character to that event? We'll talk more about this tomorrow.

Characters' Perspectives Are Shaped by Their Roles

IN THIS SESSION, you'll teach students that to deepen their understanding of characters and perspective, readers step into characters' shoes and realize that their thoughts and decisions are shaped by the times in which they live and their roles.

GETTING READY

✔ Review the strands "Analyzing Parts of a Story in Relation to the Whole" and "Analyzing Perspective" from the Reading Learning Progression.

✔ Display and revisit the passage from *Number the Stars*, Chapter 1, page 2 (in which the German soldier orders, "*Halte!*") possibly using a document camera or whiteboard (see Teaching).

✔ Display and revisit passages from *Number the Stars*, Chapter 1, pages 8–10 (see Active Engagement).

✔ Display and add to the Bend I anchor chart "Readers of Historical Fiction . . ." (see Link). 👏

✔ Make sure students have individual copies of the Narrative Reading Learning Progression. They will use two strands of this to self-assess (see Mid-Workshop Teaching). 👏

✔ Provide students with child-facing rubrics for "Inferring About Characters" and "Determining Themes/Cohesion" (see Share). 👏

✔ Provide children with copies of a fourth-grade student exemplar (see Share). 👏

✔ Have students' preassessment work ready to hand back to them (see Share).

ONE WAY that we have raised the level of students' reading over the last year has been to help children pay closer attention to perspective. You'll teach your children, for example, to ask: "Who is telling the story? Whose point of view does the reader get when reading this book?" You will want to help your students become accustomed to asking and answering those questions—point out that if they know whose inner thoughts are revealed to the reader, this can help them know the story's point of view.

But understanding perspective can become far more complex. In this session, you teach students to use their knowledge of the historical setting ("What kind of place is this?") and of the historical timeline to help understand why characters act, think, feel, and make choices as they do. The big thing you will teach is that when a character makes a choice or acts in ways that students think are "crazy," chances are good that the choice or the action makes sense in context. Readers who understand point of view are accustomed to thinking about how the historical context shapes the people living in it.

In this session, you situate this lesson into an excerpt in *Number the Stars* (although you could substitute *Rose Blanche*). Your goal is to continue to develop the notion that elements in a story (and in life) are interrelated. Reading well involves seeking to understand a character's actions and decisions, and often this requires synthesis, meaning that readers put together different aspects of the story. Synthesis work includes understanding that when characters act in ways that seem incomprehensible, the context may provide an explanation.

There is a big payoff for doing this sort of thinking. Your students will come to see that actions and choices that at first seem unremarkable are, when viewed through the lens of history, remarkable.

Characters' Perspectives Are Shaped by Their Roles
Point of View Matters

CONNECTION

Point out that coming to know a character means coming to know layers of that person, including, in historical fiction, how the historical context affects his or her thoughts and decisions.

"Readers, I know that last night you thought about why two of your characters responded differently to one thing that happens in the story, or in history. You are thinking more deeply about what influences your characters feelings and decisions. Characters start off as mere names, but as we read, we get to know them well enough that we get why they act as they do.

"Think about someone that you have gotten to know over time. Bit by bit, you got to know more layers. You first learned the outside of the person, and then you learned the inside—what he (or she) hopes for and is afraid of. Eventually you come to understand what makes that person tick."

Tell the story of a child who tried to make sense of his character's choices by considering the historical backdrop in his book.

"When you read historical fiction, it's important to remember that the times were different then. The ways characters act and feel are shaped by the times. Recently, I was listening in as the Dust Bowl club discussed the part of *Bud, Not Buddy* in which Bud, who is only ten years old, plans to sneak on a passing freight train so he can move to a new town. Kwami said, 'I think Bud is sort of a bad kid, because he should be going to school, not jumping on trains.' A reasonable thought.

"Then Jack reminded his club to think about those times, of the historical context. He said, 'I disagree because this story happens in the Depression, when lots of people were dying, they were so poor. I don't think Bud is goofing off just because he's not at school. He's trying to find his father. I think he is doing the grown-up thing.'

"Listening to Jack, I thought, *Wow*. It is smart to read and be aware that the timeline, the events in a person's life, like in Bud's life (I put out one arm), are influenced by the timeline, the events, in history (I put out the other arm). But to put those two together—to suggest that the character's timeline interweaves with the historical timeline (I twisted my arms together) is brilliant!"

While reading historical fiction involves learning about the sort of large-scale event that is apt to be reported in the newspaper, it also involves learning the smaller stories that combine to form the life of a person through those events. The smaller stories aren't usually reported by historians.

When you have a conference with a reader or club that might benefit most readers, use it for a minilesson. Your readers will be delighted that you are using them as an example, and the rest of the class is more keen to learn from each other than from you! All of this lifts the level of engagement.

Name the teaching point.

"Today I want to teach you that a character's feelings and decisions are influenced by the character's world, and his or her role in that world. When a character responds differently than you would, it helps to ask why. And to realize that the character's perspective is shaped by the times."

TEACHING

Return to a familiar scene from the read-aloud, this time thinking about *why* a character behaves as he or she does. Think about a character's actions in a way that first ignores historical context, then correct yourself.

"Let's reread the scene from the first chapter of *Number the Stars*, to investigate this work," I said, displaying the text from page 2. "Remember the moment when the German soldier orders, '*Halte!*' as Annemarie and Ellen are running and laughing down the street?"

Play acting a bit, I said, "When we first read this, it seemed odd that Annemarie said she found the word *stop*, or *halte*, frightening. When I was a kid and the school crossing guards told me to walk, not run, maybe I was embarrassed, but I wasn't *frightened!* What about you—does it make sense that Annemarie is frightened by those soldiers calling *stop*?

"Let's think about Annemarie's reaction, remembering today's teaching point." I directed students to where I'd written it. "Hmm, . . . I guess this is one of those places where it helps to ask 'Why?' I was picturing the crossing guards and policemen I've grown up with, but let's try to think about the times in which Annemarie lived. Talk to your partner about what you are thinking."

I listened in to a few kids, then said, "You are pointing out these aren't friendly neighborhood guards. They are soldiers from an enemy army who have occupied her town. They carry guns." Looking at the text, I said, "Let's see what it says," and then said, "This part says they had 'two sets of cold eyes.' I am also thinking that war is brewing, and ominous clues are everywhere about how Jewish people are being treated. So it begins to make sense that those Nazi soldiers are frightening to Annemarie and Ellen.

"Do you see that especially when you think, 'I would never do that,' it helps to step outside of your own perspectives to imagine the perspectives of the characters?"

ACTIVE ENGAGEMENT

Challenge children to do similar work, on a later part of the scene, noticing the various perspectives of several characters on the same event.

"Readers, try doing this on your own. I'll read aloud another part of that chapter—right after the soldiers have asked the girls why they are running, when Annemarie and Kirsti are back in their apartment, talking to their mother and to

As the books your children read become more complex, it will become more challenging to understand what drives or motivates characters. Characters in these stories experience pressures from many sources. Some will be personal, some related to historical events. You want your students to think hard about what influences a character's point of view, about why the character does the things they do.

Exaggerate. You are posing a challenge. You don't really think it was odd for these girls to be frightened, but you are setting the kids up to talk about why their fear makes sense, in context. You are purposely looking at the event from a modern perspective, hoping that students will see that your read of the girls' reaction doesn't make sense, since these are German soldiers, not school crossing guards.

By asking students to compare the differences between Kirsti and Mrs. Rosen's responses, you make this activity easier. Their responses are diametrically different. You are teaching perspective as well as synthesis. The differing reactions of each character to the same event are fueled by their different perspectives, their different points of view.

Ellen's mother. As I read, pay close attention to the different ways that each character responds to the retelling of the interaction with the soldiers. Notice especially how Kirsti and Mrs. Rosen respond." Gesturing to the final section of the teaching point, I said, "Remember our teaching point is that it helps to ask 'Why?' and to consider what is shaping these characters' perspectives.

"Students, remember that in this scene, Mrs. Johansen has just told Ellen's mother that the German soldiers must be on edge due to recent activities by the Danish Resistance fighters. Annemarie knows from listening in on her parents that Resistance fighters were brave Danish people who worked secretly to bring harm to the Nazis and their trucks, cars, and factories.

"As you listen, readers, remember these characters are all alive at the same time, in the same town. They are reacting to the same incident. But they behave differently! Why?"

> "I must go and speak to Ellen," Mrs. Rosen said, moving toward the door. "You girls walk a different way to school tomorrow. Promise me, Annemarie. And Ellen will promise, too."
>
> "We will, Mrs. Rosen. But what does it matter? There are German soldiers on every corner."
>
> "They will remember your faces," Mrs. Rosen said, turning in the doorway to the hall. "It is important to be one of the crowd, always. Be one of many. Be sure that they never have reason to remember your face." She disappeared into the hall and closed the door behind her.
>
> "He'll remember my face, Mama," Kirsti announced happily, "because he said I look like his little girl. He said I was pretty."
>
> "If he has such a pretty little girl, why doesn't he go back to her like a good father?" Mrs. Johansen murmured, stroking Kirsti's cheek. "Why doesn't he go back to his own country?"

"What do you notice about Kirsti's response? How is it different than Mrs. Rosen's? Why the difference?"

As children talked, I circulated, listening in on their conversations. Most kids grasped that Mrs. Rosen, who is Jewish, was frantic that the girls not be singled out by the soldiers and terrified about the harm that might come to them. Young Kirsti, though, seemed oblivious—happy that the soldier had liked her face, and proud that he'd called her pretty. She didn't understand what was going on historically and therefore had no reason to be fearful.

"Readers, eyes up here. You are saying that people respond differently—but why? What influences each of them? Think about the characters' ages, their religions, their roles, their knowledge of world events. Perhaps Mrs. Rosen has more reason to be fearful than Annemarie and Kirsti."

Recap in a way that highlights the larger point.

"Readers, when we first read this chapter, I remember thinking, 'I wouldn't have stopped running down the sidewalk just because two men told me to halt!' But when we think about the way the personal timeline of events intersects with the historical timeline, we realize these soldiers are not just crossing guards, warning us to be safe. There is a sense of

Of course, you know that the Rosens are Jewish, so Mrs. Rosen's response is influenced by that perspective. As a Jewish mother, she is devastated that the German soldiers looked her daughter Ellen in the eye, noticing her. She believes, correctly, that tensions are escalating, and that the encounter is an ominous sign. By suggesting that she may have something to fear, you set children up to anticipate the impending trouble.

Meanwhile little Kirsti has been protected from understanding what is happening in the world. She also doesn't remember a time before the soldiers were there, so she thinks of them as a normal part of life. Her innocence will play a big role in the story.

Annemarie is on the verge of understanding the Nazi threat. This is important to the story because it foreshadows what is to come. Also, the story teaches that it is harder to be brave when you understand the risks. As Annemarie's understanding of the Nazis increases, so, too, does the pressure on her.

danger during this time—by 1943 when this story occurs, World War II is raging around the globe, the Jews are being persecuted, and the soldiers play a role in this.

"When we read another chapter in *Number the Stars* later today, I know you'll listen differently. You'll be alert for how the different characters have different relationships to—and understandings of—ongoing world events. And you will want to bring this same awareness of particular characters' relationships to the setting to the book that your club is reading together, and to all the historical fiction you ever read."

LINK

Remind students that when characters act differently than expected, it helps to ask *why* and to consider whether the historical events are helping to shape these characters.

"Readers, you learned something powerful today. Whenever you read books about people living in times or situations that are different from yours, it is important to consider what influences shaped *their* perspectives at that time, to ask, 'Why would *this* character react *that* way?' Remember that a character is shaped by his or her history. Usually when characters act differently in response to the same event, this reflects differences in factors like their age, their position, their understanding of their world.

"Let's add these points to our chart," I said.

ANCHOR CHART

Readers of Historical Fiction . . .

- Read analytically, studying parts that clue them in to the facts, feelings, or setting
- Collect and organize key facts: *who, what, where, when, why, how*
- Figure out the main character's timeline and the historical timeline
- **Realize that a character's perspective is shaped by the times and by his/her roles**

FIG. 4–1 Joseph thinks analytically at the start of his book about how the historical setting affects the characters.

Realize that a character's perspective is shaped by the times and by his/her roles

Coach into Students' Reading as Well as into Their Clubs

AS THIS FIRST BEND comes to a close, you may find yourself working with individual readers to help them do the work you have taught. You'll find yourself revisiting essentials as well as recent work.

Coach into students' reading: Their volume, their comprehension

By now, all your clubs should be into their second or even third historical fiction book. If they are progressing more slowly through their shared books, hopefully they are also reading other books on the side. Sometimes, though, club members have been doing so much writing and talking that the volume of their reading slips dramatically. Suggest they set volume goals and decrease their writing about reading for a bit.

If a club is reading a book that is a bit hard, help club members track the storyline. Since I knew *Out of the Dust*, for example, would be a challenge for a club, I suggested that when they lost hold of comprehension they should go back to those confusing parts and read them aloud, discussing them. The goal of monitoring for sense might seem low level, and you may think, "Isn't that goal more apt at the start of the year?" You will find, however, that your children need to be reminded to do that skill work.

Of course, if your readers are like the Dust Bowl club readers and working with texts at levels R and beyond, it is important for you to tell them that if the book seems confusing, this doesn't necessarily mean the book is too hard. I've told students that texts are often constructed like a puzzle, and readers are meant to struggle to see how the pieces go together. They may need to hold a confusing part in mind and read on, trusting that in time that part will snap into place with the rest of the story.

Help readers do it all: Basic comprehension *and* deeper thinking may require rereading.

You'll find that some students focus so much on thinking between the historical timeline and characters' actions that they neglect to follow the storyline. When I sat by Kadija, for example, she was writing a response to Chapter 8 of *Autumn Street*. I scanned her entry and noticed she'd written about the relationship between the young protagonist, Elizabeth, and the historical context.

I asked Kadija to walk me through her thinking, so she showed me her work on the relationship between the characters and the setting. She was excited by this idea, explaining that though parents may want to protect kids from the truth, these efforts never work, and kids can handle the bad stuff. As we talked, I realized the storyline itself was confusing to her. She'd missed the critical point of a character's death.

I complimented Kadija on noticing that Elizabeth, like Kirsti, in *Number the Stars*, was being shielded from knowledge of the war because of her age. Then, shifting toward the teaching part of my conference, I asked Kadija to pat her head. She looked surprised, but when I did this, she did, too. I stopped patting my head, and then I rubbed

MID-WORKSHOP TEACHING
Readers Use Learning Progressions to Meet Expectations

"Readers, today ends this bend in the unit. After this, you're going to be working on learning life lessons from these beautiful books. You have fifteen more minutes to read, and then I'm going to ask you to also steal a moment to write a new Post-it or select one you've already written, that shows you have learned about the important work we started with on the learning progression. Get out your rubric for 'Analyzing Perspective' and for 'Analyzing Parts of a Text in Relation to the Whole,' and reread the expectations for fourth grade." I gave them a few minutes to do this work. "Before you meet with your clubs, make sure you have evidence of fourth-grade-level work in one of these strands."

my stomach, asking her to do likewise. Then I said, "When you read, the challenge is to pat your head *and* rub your stomach at the same time. You need to do several kinds of thinking at once."

I explained that it seemed that she'd done great work getting onto one line of thinking, but that she'd dropped her effort to put the whole story together into the plotline, tracking important events, like the death of one of the neighbors. I suggested because the book is so complex, she might need to read with one idea in mind—patting her head—and to reread, with the other work foremost (rubbing her stomach). I then channeled her to reread, trying to recall all the main events happening in the story.

Readers Take Stock to Pinpoint How Their Work Can Get Stronger

Ask students to use a learning progression and a student exemplar to assess their own work and crystallize new goals.

"Clubs, I'm returning your performance assessments to you—our work with *Blizzard*—and will you look between the thinking you did for the questions about analyzing perspective and part to whole on that, and your latest work? Talk about how you've changed, saying things like, "I used to do . . . as a reader, but now I . . ." Then help each other do even better work so we can create a celebratory bulletin board of your best thinking—and be ready for new challenges in the next bend."

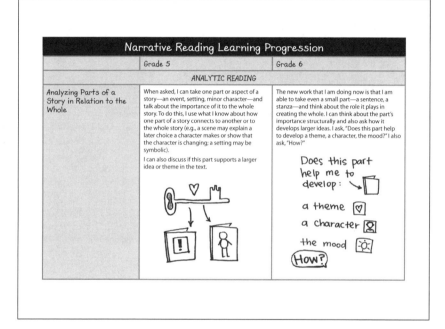

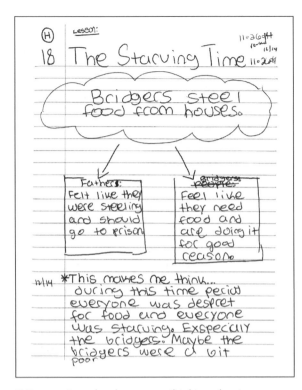

FIG. 4–2 Sam develops some thinking about perspective, including how the time period affects characters' thinking.

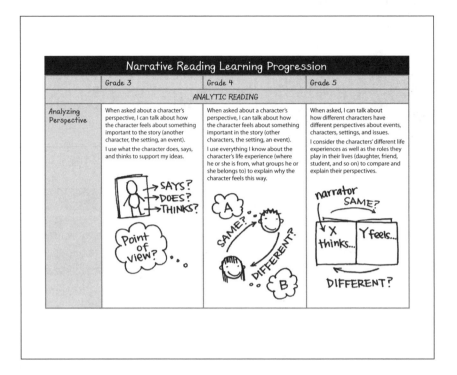

 # CHARACTERS' PERSPECTIVES ARE SHAPED BY THEIR ROLES

Readers, today, you set goals for yourself. You'll want to decide, tonight, whether to read on or to reread, but either way, do some writing and thinking about your reading that shows your new goals. Annotate your writing, too, with marginal notes that name what you are trying to do.

Making Significance

IN THIS SESSION, you'll teach students that strong readers read complex texts alertly, poised to interpret as they read. To do this, they recognize when a passage is significant and think about how that passage connects to other parts of the text, and figure out what it is *really* saying.

GETTING READY

✔ Prior to this session, read aloud Chapter 3 of *Number the Stars*.

✔ Be prepared to return to Chapter 10 of *The Tiger Rising* or another passage from a favorite read-aloud. You'll want to choose an excerpt that illustrates what you mean by saying that some passages seem to have been written in bold (see Connection).

✔ Prepare to read aloud a passage from *Number the Stars*, Chapter 3 (see Teaching).

✔ Display the chart "Clues that Suggest a Passage Is Worth Pondering" (see Teaching).

✔ Prepare to distribute a copy of another passage to one member of each club (see Active Engagement).

✔ Display and update the anchor chart "Historical Fiction Readers . . ." (see Link).

✔ Display a chart from Unit 1 *Interpreting Characters*, "Thought Prompts to Help Us Move from Simple to Complex Ideas" (see Mid-Workshop Teaching).

✔ Display the chart "Growing Powerful Book Club Conversations" (see Share).

✔ Provide giant Post-its to send home with children (see Homework).

TODAY'S SESSION starts a bend that is devoted to helping students determine themes, one of the strands on the Narrative Reading Learning Progression. You will teach readers that big ideas do not emerge out of looking up in the air and trying to discern meaningful insights. They instead emerge from close, attentive readings of texts. Roy Peter Clark describes this process of grounding big ideas in concrete details as moving up and down a ladder of abstraction. Readers need to know that it is from the details that bigger thinking develops, and once the reader has an insight, he or she returns to details to consolidate this thinking.

When children first work on interpreting as they read, they almost seem to hope the author will come right out and say, "*This* passage supports the idea that. . . ." Skillful authors don't write that explicitly, though. The ideas that a text advances are hidden in all sorts of small details that together, suggest bigger meaning. And never does the author say, "And all this shows. . . ." It is important, therefore, to teach readers to read closely, trusting that the details and the language in a text are important. The close reader will note that at times, certain parts of a story *do* seem to call to the reader, almost as if they are shouting, "Here, right here, this part is extra significant!" Sometimes, it's when a symbol is repeated. Other times, the inner thinking or dialogue of a character suggests an epiphany. And still other times, certain actions suggest that characters have changed—these are all pivotal narrative moments that cry out for interpretation.

For today's session, you will teach children to pause especially at passages that, as you'll put it, "seem to be written in bold letters." You are saying that readers pay attention, and to do this, push a metaphorical pause button when things seem laden with meaning. Readers pause to think hard not only about what is happening in the book but also about what it all means.

Making Significance

CONNECTION

Remind readers of times in an earlier unit when the read-aloud book seemed to ask readers to pause and interpret.

"Readers, I'm sure you remember how, when we were reading *The Tiger Rising*, there were certain parts of the book that begged us to pause and to pay close attention—parts that seemed like windows to some deeper meaning at the heart of the whole story. Thumbs up if you remember the part when Willie May told Rob she thought his rash was really sadness, wanting to come out, being kept in." I reread part of the familiar passage from *The Tiger Rising:*

> "I can tell you how to cure that," said Willie May, pointing with her cigarette at his legs. "I can tell you right now. Don't need to go to no doctor."
>
> "Huh?" said Rob. He stopped chewing his gum and held his breath. What if Willie May healed him and then he had to go back to school?
>
> "Sadness," said Willie May, closing her eyes and nodding her head. "You keeping all that sadness down low, in your legs. You not letting it get up to your heart, where it belongs. You got to let that sadness rise on up."

❧ Name the teaching point.

"Today I want to teach you that readers don't wait for someone else to decide which passages are worth pausing over. Readers read alertly, poised to say, 'Wow. This part almost seems like it's written in bold.' Readers then ask, 'How does this connect to *other* parts of the text?' and 'What is this part *really* about?'"

TEACHING

Read the class read-aloud, pausing when students signal that a passage seems to have been written in bold.

"I'm going to read on in *Number the Stars*. If we reach a passage that seems like it's been written in bold, will you signal with a raised thumb? Then we'll ask those questions: 'Does this connect to earlier parts of the text?' and 'What's this

◆ COACHING

There is nothing sacrosanct about this particular passage, and your point only makes sense if that passage did make an impression on your students earlier—if it didn't, choose another.

You could instead open this lesson by asking students to recall times when they have seen a movie and found places in the film where the entire room seemed to be holding its breath because something really important was happening. Those are the parts when, even if viewers really have to go to the bathroom, they don't dream of leaving the theater, because they can't miss one minute. There are places like that in novels, too.

Readers won't all pause at the same parts of a text. Although some passages will be so multi-layered and striking that no reader could pass them by, your job is not to guide students to select the "right" passage so much as to help them read, aware that some portions of a text are worth considering more deeply.

part *really* about? 'You'll find that authors have ways to signal that a passage is worth pondering," I said, gesturing toward a chart.

"Okay, I'll start reading and I'll go for a page or so before we pause, so that we get into the story and have some text to work with. After I've read a bit, signal if I come to one of those pause-worthy spots." I read an excerpt from Chapter 3 of *Number the Stars*.

> Annemarie was almost asleep when there was a light knock on the bedroom door. Candlelight appeared as the door opened, and her mother stepped in.
>
> "Are you asleep, Annemarie?"
>
> "No. Why? Is something wrong?"
>
> "Nothing's wrong. But I'd like you to get up and come out to the living room. Peter's here. Papa and I want to talk to you."
>
> Annemarie jumped out of bed, and Kirsti grunted in her sleep. Peter! She hadn't seen him in a long time. There was something frightening about him being here at night.

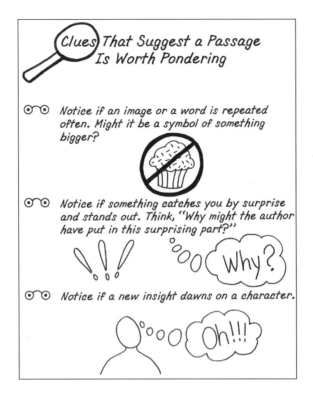

I continued to read aloud the passage about Peter's surprise visit and how Annemarie was delighted to see him, even though his visits these days were hurried and almost secretive. On this night, Peter had brought some special gifts, including the two seashells he carried in his pocket. But then, Papa had something serious to tell Annemarie.

> "For your mama and papa, I brought something more practical. Two bottles of beer!"
>
> Mama and Papa smiled and raised their glasses. Papa took a sip and wiped the foam from his upper lip. Then his face became more serious.
>
> "Annemarie," he said. "Peter tells us that the Germans have issued orders closing many stores run by Jews."
>
> "Jews?" Annemarie repeated. "Is Mrs. Hirsch Jewish? Is that why the button shop is closed? Why have they done that?"
>
> Peter leaned forward. "It is their way of tormenting. For some reason, they want to torment Jewish people. It has happened in other countries. They have taken their time here—have let us relax a little. But now it seems to be starting."

One of your goals here is to move your fourth-graders into deeper interpretive work even when they have just read a little of a text. You'll see on the "Determining Themes/Cohesion" strand of the learning progression that the big new work for fourth-graders involves not waiting until the end of the story to read interpretively. Here, you nudge your readers toward this work by reminding them to pay attention to significant parts when the story calls out for them to do that.

Remember that important passages often link to earlier passages. The gift of seashells is suggestive of Kirsti's longing for summer vacations by the seashore. The mention of seashells also highlights the fact that Copenhagen is near the ocean, with Sweden across the water, which will become important to this story. Still, I didn't decide to pause here because only a few children gestured that they saw the gift as talkworthy. There is an overwhelming urge to teach students the significance that we as adult readers see. Remember that you want to teach kids a process for interpreting more than you want to teach them your interpretations. Once there is more repetition and more emphasis on certain things—the sea, the pink cupcakes—even young readers will notice them and then they can look back with you and see more than they originally saw in this passage.

"But why the button shop? What harm is a button shop? Mrs. Hirsch is such a nice lady. Even Samuel—he's a dope, but he would never harm anyone. How could he—he can't even see, with his thick glasses!"

Then Annemarie thought of something else. "If they can't sell their buttons, how will they earn a living?"

"Friends will take care of them," Mama said gently. "That's what friends do."

When children signal that the text seems to be written in bold, nudge them to ask, "How does this passage connect with earlier ones?" and "What does this *really* mean?"

I noticed some children signaling to stop, and I agreed. Pausing, I reread just the last bit: "'Friends will take care of them . . . That's what friends do.'" Referencing the teaching point, I said, "Remember that when readers reach passages that seem like they've been written in bold, they think, 'How does this connect to earlier parts of the text?' and 'What is this part *really* about?'"

ACTIVE ENGAGEMENT

Distribute copies of another potent passage to one child from each club, asking that child to read aloud and for the club to signal for the reader to pause when the text seems to be "written in bold." Then clubs can talk.

Distributing another passage to children dotting the meeting area, I said, "Readers, let's keep reading. Let's look at another passage that seems like it's written in bold, that beckons for readers to pause and interpret." I'd marked the passage that began, "Then Annemarie thought of something else. 'If they can't sell buttons, how will they earn a living?'" I said, "Will one person from each club continue reading aloud where I left off, and when the book reaches a place that feels important, call, 'Stop and talk.' Then, all of you, talk about what this passage—and the one before it—is really about."

After children read for a bit, if they hadn't yet paused, I signaled for them to do so. As clubs talked together about the passage they'd just read aloud to each other, I said in a voiceover, "I'm remembering back to earlier parts of the book, aren't you?" I reread a sentence or two from the text from Chapter 3, which the children had heard earlier in read-aloud, and left more time for children to talk.

Annemarie and Ellen exchanged looks that meant: Kirsti is so dumb. No one in Copenhagen had taken a vacation at the seashore since the war began. There were no pink-frosted cupcakes; there hadn't been for months.

Read this part with great significance, almost imbuing your voice with bolds, knowing that this will channel many readers to signal that this is a good stopping place. You may decide to pick up your pen, saying, "I'm going to jot for a minute to get my mind going—will you do the same?" If you do that, you can scrawl furiously, intent on the page, hoping students will follow suit. The only sound will be the scratch of pens. But the read-aloud passages are long enough that you may decide this lengthens the minilesson too much.

FIG. 5–1 Some of your readers will jot in order to develop thinking, or to record their thinking. Keep an eye on children whose writing is taking so much time that it interferes with their reading. For these children, have them only jot when it really helps them get to deeper thinking.

LINK

Remind students of the repertoire of work they might do as they read.

"Club members, before you disperse, will you remind one another of the goalpost page for today's reading? Later today, you'll have time to meet in clubs and to share the passages you notice and your responses to them. And of course, there are many things you've learned to do as readers of historical fiction that you may find yourself doing today again, as you read," I gestured to the charts we'd been making across the unit, and updated the anchor chart.

ANCHOR CHART

Readers of Historical Fiction . . .

- Read analytically, studying parts that clue them in to the facts, feelings of setting
- Collect and organize key facts: who, what, where, when, why, how
- Keep track of the major character's timeline, the historical timeline, and how they intersect
- Realize that a character's perspective is shaped by the times and by his/her roles
- **Determine themes and support them with evidence from across the story**

Determine themes and support them with evidence from across the story

Coaching Readers Toward Goals, Including the Goal of Thoughtful Conversations

AT THE START OF TODAY, readers will be reading independently as you confer with them. You'll want to carry the learning progressions with you and to be aware of the goals that you have for individual readers. Is one reader especially apt to mumble over challenging words? If so, remember that even though this is a unit on historical fiction, it is still a reading unit, and your goals for readers are always relevant. You may ask a reader to clue you in to what's happening in a story and to share what she thinks will happen next, and then you might press for a prediction, drawing on all the instruction readers have ever received in predicting.

Of course, later today your students will meet in clubs—and if you wish, you can ask one club to talk during reading time so that you can listen in on more conversations. As you listen to members of clubs talk, keep in mind that there is one pattern that marks less successful clubs—ones where the talk flags. In those clubs, readers come to the table with their ideas in hand almost as if the ideas were a small pile of playing cards, and then readers lay out one card after another, often in round-robin fashion. The conversations are more about reporting on ideas developed prior to meeting rather than growing ideas in conversation.

In the most successful book clubs, however, the move to lay down one's cards is a preliminary move, and there comes a time when one card is moved front and center so that the whole group talks back and forth about that one card, that one idea. When a club changes from presenting premade ideas to actually discussing each other's thoughts, the conversation comes to life.

Once children focus on a selected idea, they can begin developing ideas together.

Listen to the conversations your clubs have about books. Chances are good that unless you have taught children otherwise, you'll find that in one club after the next, their conversations jump from topic to topic. Luckily, the problem is easily addressed, and changing this can be transformative.

Here's how I tackled this issue with the Freedom Fighters club. This group was halfway through *Roll of Thunder, Hear My Cry*. When I approached Aly, who had emerged as a club leader, she was presenting a plan of action. I admired her decision to have a procedural conversation before jumping into content, listening in as she said, "How about if we begin and everyone says their best passage and their best idea? Then we can talk? We could go in a circle."

Often, when five ideas are laid out in sequence, they tend to glom together, losing their distinctiveness. Also, the process of five kids, each laying out an idea, eats up time. I prefer that the club say, "Who has a passage you think is particularly important and an idea you are excited about?" and begin with just those selections. But I withheld my comments to let the club gain momentum and to give myself time to decide what the most important intervention might be.

Josh jumped in first, saying, "Well, I noticed that Cassie stands up for her rights. It's like she isn't aware of how unsafe the world is for blacks."

"I noticed almost the same," Fallon said. "Cassie seems really brave. Especially since whites have so much power, and they can get away with seriously hurting black people. Like when they burned the Berry men and there wasn't *one* punishment for that. Cassie *still* insists on being treated fairly, she still stands up for her rights."

I was already impressed. Yes, the children were laying out their ideas, like one might lay out playing cards. But Fallon had seen that her idea resembled Josh's—suggesting she was thinking about his idea, and thinking across ideas. Often children can repeat each other without seeming in the least bit aware they are doing so. I was also impressed that Fallon didn't just say, "My idea is the same. Ditto." Instead, she reiterated the initial idea, embellishing on it.

Over the next few minutes, one child after another added his or her thoughts about the Logan family. Aly piped in, "I noticed that sometimes being quiet is the better way

"Readers, last weekend, I was invited to a pot luck dinner . . . but I forgot about it until the very last minute so I didn't have time to make a casserole or a blueberry pie. It was a Sunday so the stores were closed, so I just ended up bringing a bag of napkins and plastic spoons. When I arrived and saw everyone else carrying in their steaming casserole pots and I just had a plastic bag with napkins in it, I was so mortified.

So readers, what I want to tell you is that a book club is like a potluck dinner, and bringing a little package of napkins just doesn't cut it! In the same way, you have a responsibility to bring something to your club that will help your club have a fantastic literary conversation. In a few minutes, you'll have time to meet with your clubs. You've been noting passages that feel as if they've been written in bold. Will you take a minute to rehearse your best thinking about these passages? You might find these thought prompts helpful," I said, as I gestured to a chart.

After children had time to reread and to think, I channeled them to launch into conversations with their club mates.

Thought Prompts to Help Us Grow Complex Ideas

★ Could this have anything to do with...?

★ I wonder...

★ Maybe...

★ Remember earlier in the story when...

★ These ideas might go together...

★ The author might be trying to teach us ...

to go. Like Mr. Morrison and Big Ma keep the family safe by kind of hushing people, or taking them away from fights. But Cassie and Uncle Hammer are always ready to fight, and that doesn't work so well."

Isaac said, "The thing I noticed is just how unfair things are for the Logans and all the black people."

"Back then, your color mattered," Sam added, again talking in response to one of his classmates' comments. He added, "The book takes place about fifty or sixty years ago. Even though black people weren't slaves, they *had* been slaves not that long before."

I knew I could comment on a pattern—even when the club had decided to just do a round-robin presentation of ideas, they were relating what one person said to what others had said, responding to each other in impressive ways. But now Sam said, "How about if we put our ideas, our Post-its, into my hat and then we draw one Post-it from the hat and have a long talk about that one?" The kids had clearly done this before, and they began this familiar process.

At this point I leaned in and said, "Can I stop you for a moment?"

Teach students to ask, "Why?"

I complimented them on having the rhythm down for how book conversations often go. They collected ideas for a bit and then knew to settle down to discuss one idea in more depth. But I said, "In conversations, just like in writing, it is important to pick a subject *that matters*. So after you have laid out a few possible things to talk about, rather than picking one out of a hat, you're better off to step back and ask, 'Which of these is going to take us to new and deeper thinking?' Deciding what to talk about is as important as deciding on passages that seem like they've been written in bold—it is a big deal.

"To make the decision about what to talk about, remember your goals. Earlier, your club decided to think more deeply about characters. And here's my second tip: When you want to deepen your thinking about characters—about almost any idea, really—it usually helps to ask, '*Why?*' Like that question, '*Why* did Jeremy treat the Logans differently?' But you could also ask, '*Why* is Cassie so brave? *Why* might Mama, Big Ma, and Mr. Morrison hush people—and the others, like Uncle Hammer, handle this differently? What's at stake if they don't hush protests?' Could you try taking a why question and thinking about it?"

"Yes," the group answered simultaneously.

Soon the club was engrossed in conversation about *why* Jeremy is so nice to the Logans. Before moving on, I said, "You've said that he especially wants to be friends with Stacey—but still, why? Keep asking that question and your thinking will get deeper." Then, I said, "Let me give you a last tip for today: When you're trying to understand something, say, 'Could it be . . .' and throw out ideas. And remember, the author doesn't always tell you things right out, but she does give you *telling* details. They're on the page, waiting for you to take note."

Readers Can Use an Artifact to Provide a Focal Point for Conversation

Encourage students to use an additional strategy to ground their thinking and improve the quality of their club discussions.

After listening to club conversations for a while and coaching into those conversations, I asked for the class's attention. "Readers, I've been hearing a lot of thoughtful conversations. I want to add one more idea to your repertoire of strategies. It is this: Conversations often go better if you put an artifact in the middle of the table and the whole group looks closely at that one thing. An artifact might be one person's idea that your whole club agrees is important. Or it might be a passage from part of the book that all of you want to return to. Or perhaps it's an entry that you've written about that passage.

"The main thing is—rather than jump from idea to idea, it's often helpful if your club zooms in on one idea to linger on together. For today, I suggest you actually put a part that seems significant in front of you, take some time to reread it, and then remember when you talk to reference that passage. Go back to the exact words."

I motioned for children to resume their clubs, pointing out the chart I had ready as a reminder for ways to make their book club conversations more powerful.

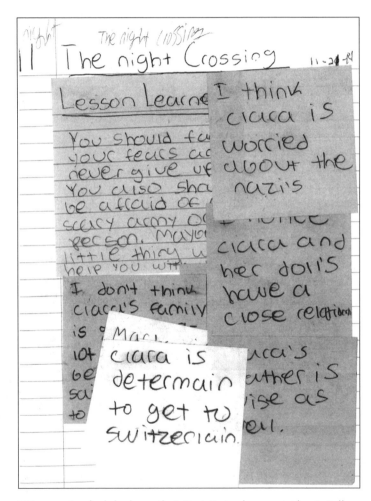

FIG. 5–2 Sam's club places their Post-its to choose an idea to talk long about.

FIND A PASSAGE THAT IS SIGNIFICANT AND USE IT TO WRITE THE BOOK'S THEME

Tonight I am sending you home with a few big, pink Post-its. On each of these pink Post-its, I want you to try capturing the big idea, the theme of the text. You'll be writing an interpretation of the text.

To do this, first read on in the text, alert to those passages that make you pause and think, "Whoa. This is significant for the whole text."

Once you have located that passage, read it two or three times, thinking hard about it. Ask questions like, "What's this story *really* about?" or "What is this author really saying—about life?" Think about how that one passage connects to others that came before it. Go back and reread those. Think, "How do these passages support an idea that is central in this story?"

Then try your hand at putting that real message—that big idea—onto one of the large pink Post-its.

If you don't encounter one of those significant passages in the pages you read tonight, go back and reread a part of the book that does feel like it's been written in bold, and do this work off that part.

We'll be talking about these ideas—about your pink Post-its—in school.

Seeing Big Ideas in Small Details

IN THIS SESSION, you'll teach students that when readers think or write about big ideas from a book, they support their ideas with small moments, small details, and small objects found in the text.

GETTING READY

✔ Prior to this session, read aloud through the end of Chapter 4 of *Number the Stars*.

✔ Plan to read aloud all of Chapter 5 in this minilesson—quickly, breathlessly, without stopping! The minilesson will run longer than usual (see Connection and Teaching and Active Engagement).

✔ Display chart "Thinking Deeply about Important Passages in a Book" (see Connection and Link).

✔ Display and add to anchor chart "Readers of Historical Fiction . . ." (see Link).

✔ "Inferring about Characters and Other Story Elements" strand of the Grade 4 Narrative Reading Learning Progression and student exemplar writing sample (see Conferring and Small-Group Work).

I N THIS SESSION, you will help your students continue learning to talk and think about the meanings in a text, this time by examining the specific details and objects in which those meanings are lodged. In doing so, you ultimately will help them understand more about the concept of symbolism. When a person has something huge and complex, rich and deep to say, often the most powerful way to convey that meaning is through tiny concrete specifics.

So often, the biggest meanings in life are conveyed through metaphor. In weddings, two people exchange rings to symbolize a never-ending commitment to each other. The first apartment key signifies more than the key to a building; it unlocks the door to adult independence.

How important it is to make sure we give ourselves, and our children, the time to have ideas! As your readers continue to build their interpretive skills, they'll realize not only in reading workshop but in the text of their lives that *the most powerful ideas are often embedded in things*, in the grit of life. In a bear, dressed in green corduroy overalls with one button missing—a bear who is nonetheless adopted and loved. In a woman knitting in the crowds, her eyes riveted to a blood-stained guillotine. Reading literature is all about understanding that we human beings do not need to choose between thinking about things, about the grit of life, and thinking about ideas, because the biggest and most complex ideas in the world are just that—lodged in the world.

So, too, the pink cupcakes that Kirsti longs for in *Number the Stars* are not just pink cupcakes, and the star necklace, imprinted on Annemarie's hand, is not just a necklace. That Star of David is a tiny thing—yet so big. Exploring the meaning of that imprint on her hand will be a way to bring children toward a study of symbolism and of abstraction—and of the relationship between gritty specifics and big ideas.

Seeing Big Ideas in Small Details

CONNECTION

Tell children that today's minilesson will proceed differently than usual. Then read an intense section of the read-aloud book, stopping at a passage that gives readers pause.

"Readers, I know that you have been reading your novels, aware that there are passages that ask readers to pause to think about the big themes in the story. And you have been writing down your big ideas." I held up a big pink Post-it, reminding students of yesterday's homework. "We'll talk about these later," I said.

"I'm going to start our minilesson by doing something unusual—I'm going to simply read to you. Eventually, you'll see why I do this. Perhaps we'll come to a place in the text that makes us pause, but then again, perhaps the text will be written in a 'Don't stop! Read on' sort of a way. Some of you may just listen while others follow along in your copies of *Number the Stars*." I opened *Number the Stars*, leaned in, and began reading.

I began to read aloud at the beginning of Chapter 5 and read on, helping readers to imagine the scene when the Nazi soldiers barged into Annemarie's family's apartment, looking for the Rosens.

> *Annemarie eased the bedroom door open quietly, only a crack, and peeked out. Behind her, Ellen was sitting up, her eyes wide.*
>
> *She could see Mama and Papa in their nightclothes, moving about. Mama held a lighted candle, but as Annemarie watched, she went to a lamp and switched it on. It was so long a time since they had dared to use the strictly rationed electricity after dark that the light in the room seemed startling to Annemarie, watching through the slightly opened bedroom door. She saw her mother look automatically to the blackout curtains, making certain that they were tightly drawn.*
>
> *Papa opened the front door to the soldiers.*
>
> *"This is the Johansen apartment?" A deep voice asked the question loudly, in the terribly accented Danish.*

I continued reading through the entire scene with the soldiers and the girls, without stopping, until I reached this passage:

COACHING

You'll read an entire chapter within this minilesson—something very unusual. Be prepared to read it swiftly and dramatically, demonstrating the sort of passionate, fast reading you do when parts of a book are written so that it is impossible to stop.

When I read aloud, I aspire for the book I am reading to be the greatest book ever in my students' lives. The books people recall as their most remarkable are often books that sizzle with intensity.

The officer tore the photograph in half and dropped the pieces on the floor. Then he turned, the heels of his shiny boots grinding into the pictures, and left the apartment. Without a word, the other two officers followed. Papa stepped forward and closed the door behind him.

Annemarie relaxed the clenched fingers of her right hand, which still clutched Ellen's necklace. She looked down, and saw that she had imprinted the Star of David into her palm.

Remind students that when readers meet passages that seem to be written in bold, they pause to ask, "What's this *really* about?" Channel students to draw on prompts to think deeply about the passage.

I looked up from the book. Kids were on their knees, leaning in toward the story. "Whoa! This is one of those important passages that feels written in bold, doesn't it?" I said, pointing to the "Thinking Deeply about Important Passages in a Book" chart. The kids nodded their heads.

"So let's pause and think about some huge questions that readers ask when they get to really important parts of a book," I said, gesturing to the chart.

"You've been asking some of these questions. So think on your own for a moment." I paused briefly. "Now turn and talk." I listened in as pairs of children talked. Lily and Jasmine discussed how friends take care of friends, connecting that idea with how Annemarie removed the Jewish star necklace from her friend Ellen's neck to protect her.

After a few minutes, I convened children's attention. "Readers, you are all discussing *big* ideas and *big* questions. Now I want to share an important bit of advice. The writer Richard Price has said, 'The bigger the issue, the smaller you write.' What he means by this is that when you are writing or thinking about big ideas, you lodge your ideas in the smallest details from the story."

❖ **Name the teaching point.**

"Today I want to teach you that when you are thinking, talking, or writing about big ideas—as you are doing today—it's wise to lodge your big ideas in small moments, small details, small objects."

TEACHING AND ACTIVE ENGAGEMENT

Rally students to cite examples of ways that big ideas from a previous read-aloud book were carried by concrete specifics.

"Let's try this for a moment by thinking about *The Tiger Rising*, just for a second. Think about the big messages, the big ideas, in that novel." I gave children a minute to do this, then gestured for some of them to call out what surfaced in their minds.

☆ Thinking Deeply About Important Passages in a Book

- What is significant about this part of the story?

- How does this part fit with an earlier part? How does it connect to what the whole story is really about?

- Why might the author have written in this particular way, including these details, words?

- What is the character learning about life, the world? What am I learning?

character → 🌍 ← me

One child piped up with, "It told about how you have to let your feelings out, not trap them in."

I nodded, taking that one response as sufficient, and pushed on. "So did Kate DiCamillo follow Richard Price's advice and use small details or small objects to carry the message that it is important to let your feelings out?" Soon the class had listed a few concrete items that represented these ideas: a suitcase, full of pain. A tiger in a cage. A rash.

Turn the class's attention to the current read-aloud and recruit them to join you in considering whether big ideas are carried in small details.

Then I said, "So now, let's think about whether there are small details or objects in *Number the Stars* that carry big ideas. If we find those objects that hold big meanings, they can be called *symbols*." I gave children time to think with me. "Are any of you thinking about the pink cupcakes?" I asked, and many children nodded. "Now we have to think about the big idea they represent. Hmm, . . . What does the book say about them?"

Soon children had piped in that Kirsti wants them and can't have them, and the class and I wondered whether those cupcakes represented things the characters couldn't have anymore.

I could, of course, have said that the cupcakes represent the innocence of Kirsti—an innocence that the war will threaten—but the goal is to support children doing this thinking. Their ideas will often start simple and they will become layered as you continue to read on.

Invite students to think and write about other big ideas in the passage you just read aloud, lodging their ideas in concrete details. Scaffold this by reading aloud a passage or two that reference key details.

"Right now, will you work with your club to think if there are other big ideas in the passage I read earlier—and then to think whether those big ideas are lodged in specific objects, in symbols. It can help to reread. I know you don't each have a copy of the book so I'll skim over it, rereading some passages out loud."

I reread the parts of the passage from Chapter 5 that highlighted important small details I hoped children would notice: the dark hair, the photograph, the candle, the blue trunk, and of course, the Star of David necklace.

You may want to starting with the line from Chapter 5 that begins, "He laughed scornfully." Continue to look for text that brings out small, significant details, and reread those passages or snippets to children.

As children talked, I voiced over, reminding them of key questions they could ask.

In one club, Jasmine said, "I would have been terrified . . . like . . ." (*she imitated being paralyzed by fear*).

I asked Jasmine and her club, "Would you have been scared like that only if you were Ellen—or also if you were Annemarie?" I expected that question would channel the members of her club to talk about the risks the Johansens were taking.

Lily chimed in. "It's not just the parents who are looking out for the Rosens. It's the kids. Like Annemarie. When Ellen can't undo that necklace 'cause her fingers are frozen up with fear, Annemarie does it; she jerks the necklace off Ellen. It must have hurt Ellen, but Annemarie was saving her. She is becoming braver and braver."

Although the children have not pointed this out yet and may not have considered it, by holding that necklace in her hand, Annemarie risks the possibility that the soldiers will mistake her for the Jewish one, so she is risking her own safety to protect her friend.

Convene the class and share some of the ideas you overheard in club conversations.

"Class, listen to the ideas that Lily and her club mates have been saying," I said, and Lily explained that she and her club mates were thinking that Annemarie was becoming braver and braver. She tore the star necklace off Ellen to save her from the Nazi soldiers.

Building on this, I said, "Readers, listen up because I have something important to say. You've each grown big ideas and linked them to something small—to an object, a moment in the story, a symbol."

LINK

Send children off to read, reminding them to mark sections that feel important and to use the anchor chart and the "Thinking Deeply about Important Passages in a Book" chart to guide their thinking.

"It's time to read your club books on your own. Think where you are in your book. Remind yourself of the different sorts of work that readers of historical fiction tend to do at the start, in the middle, and at the end of a book. Notice I added some of our new work to the chart. Just as I added reminders to our chart, you want to add these strategies to your repertoire." I gestured to the anchor chart that we'd made earlier in the unit, to which I had added our most recent strategy.

"So pause for a moment, and make a plan for your reading work today. What of this work are you doing?" I waited a moment, then added: "Remember to think in big ideas *and small concrete specifics* including details and objects. I can't wait to see the work you do. Off you go. Get to reading."

ANCHOR CHART

Readers of Historical Fiction . . .

- Read analytically, studying parts that clue them in to the facts, feelings, or setting
- Collect and organize key facts: *who, what, where, when, why, how*
- Keep track of the major character's timeline, the historical timeline, and how they intersect
- Realize that a character's perspective is shaped by the times and his/her roles
- Determine themes and support them with evidence from across the story
- **Lodge big ideas in small moments, small details, and objects**

Lodge big ideas in small moments, small details, and objects

Coach Readers Who Need Help Seeing Fine-Grained Detail

I WANT TO ASK YOU SOMETHING that I often ask teachers when I help them become stronger at conferring. "What have you been learning especially as you confer and work with small groups lately?" The question sometimes catches teachers with whom I work off guard because they think of conferences and small groups as times for *teaching* more than for *learning*. But one important way to raise the level of your work with kids is to make sure that you are learning from that work. You'll find you approach the kids differently if you intend to learn from them.

You'll want to plan on learning from your students as they are engaged in reading. To what extent can they transfer the work you did together as a class to their club books? Of course, in order to find symbols in those novels, it will help readers to do the work you supported yesterday, reading carefully for passages that feel imbued with significance.

(continues)

MID-WORKSHOP TEACHING   **Self-Assess Your Interpretation Work: Are You Doing Your Strongest Thinking?**

"Readers, eyes up here. You have more time to read, and I don't want to get in your way. But I do want you to know that in this unit of study, I'm trying to teach you a few sophisticated reading skills—so be aware of your work on those skills as you read. The first is *monitoring for sense: fitting the pieces together*. We talked about it earlier, but I am hoping you are remembering to do this. You learned how the parts of a story—the historical events and the personal events, the characters and the plot and the setting, all fit together. And not only that, you also learned that each aspect of the story influences other aspects.

"The second huge reading skill—the one I have been teaching the last few days and that you learned in an earlier unit—is *analyzing perspective*. You've investigated why characters do the things they do, how they're shaped by the roles they play and the times in which they live. The third skill you've been working on is *determining themes*. That skill can also be called *interpretation*. People interpret in life, all the time. You don't take out the trash, and your parents say, 'That shows you're not willing to do your share around here.' Your parents are taking a small action and saying it actually shows something very big. That's a simple real-life version of interpretation.

"As a fourth-grade reader, you are also expected to notice places where the author seems to want you to think about a deeper meaning or message, and you try to figure out what the author is saying about life. What life lesson is the author trying to teach?

"The other thing you are expected to do as a fourth-grade interpreter is support any of your ideas—whether those ideas are about how one part fits into the whole story or about character traits or themes. Once you get an idea, you are expected to read on, seeing evidence of that idea, or letting the text change your thinking about that idea.

"Will you think about whether you are doing this work, especially the work of supporting your ideas? This means that if you are following an idea as you read, you should be able to support that idea by citing exact details and examples from the text. Make sure you can do that. Before you read on, take a moment to self-assess, and make sure you are doing your very best thinking."

When I conferred with some of the children who had read *Sarah, Plain and Tall* earlier and were now reading *Skylark*, I was interested in understanding which aspects of the book they were taking in and which aspects they were flying past. It is a short text and rich in symbolic detail. When I asked one club member and then another to show me parts they were noticing and to retell what they'd read, it became clear that most of them weren't paying any attention to the fine-grained specifics that were critically important to understanding the books they were reading. I asked several club members whether they'd seen any significance in the passage in which Sarah, the new bride, stares for a long while at Seal, the cat, after learning that Seal is pregnant with her first litter of kittens. Papa smiles at Sarah's look, as Sarah gazes meaningfully at Seal and then breaks into a smile, saying, "Kittens" with a smile, "Kittens." That is the last word in the chapter. No, none of the members of that club thought that passage was important in the least.

My question, then, was how to help them to attend to details such as that one. I directed Lily's attention back to the passage about the pregnant cat and asked her what she thought was going on. She looked at me blankly and retold the sequential plotline. I tried to push a bit, asking, "What's *really* going on here?" but Lily looked at me curiously. "Sarah is happy for the cat. She probably likes kittens." I tried again. "Lily,

in the books you are reading now, details matters. The author doesn't put a detail like this into a scene unless there is some bigger message behind the detail. So think again about why the pregnant cat is in this story. There's Sarah, newly married to Papa. She's looking at the cat, who is going to have kittens, and Sarah starts smiling. Now, what might this mean?"

Almost at once, Lily started to jump up and down in her chair. "She's going to have a baby, too!" she shouted. "Or she thinks she is. And she's happy!"

It doesn't matter whether Lily picks up on *this particular* detail. What matters, rather, is that Lily and other readers understand that details are in stories for reasons. Lily's club became enthralled with the idea that they could figure out parts of the story that the main character (in this story, Anna, Papa's daughter) hadn't yet figured out.

To help readers pay attention to detail, you might remind them of the "Inferring about Characters and Other Story Elements" strand of the Grade 4 Narrative Reading Learning Progression and the student work that illustrates it, asking them to look between their current work and the learning progression.

Readers Study How Ordinary Objects Often Symbolize Big Ideas

Help students go from talking about important objects to talking about those objects as symbols.

"I'm noticing, Readers, that many of you are finding symbols (recurring images, objects, and details) in your books, just as earlier you did in *The Tiger Rising* and now in *Number the Stars*. And you are right that just as pink cupcakes are symbols in *Number the Stars*—representing everything the kids can't have anymore and maybe even symbolizing the loss of those early, carefree times, so too, your books have tons of symbols too.

"Right now, will you think about a symbol you have found in one of your club books—it needn't be the book you are reading now, it could be your first book. Then leaf through the pages so that you find a passage where that symbol is lodged."

I gave children a few minutes to do this. "Will you stop and jot, for just a few minutes, what you are thinking about that symbol?" As the children jotted, I moved among them, noticing that many of them were talking about objects that were important to a story, but that they weren't really talking about the objects as symbols.

I convened the class. "Readers, many of you are talking about certain objects. I'm going to remind you how you can actually talk about those details or objects as symbols. Let's do that work with Emma's writing, first," and I read aloud Emma's entry.

"Class, do you see that Emma has listed why the objects in her book are important to Rifka, the heroine who is alone, trying to immigrate to America—she said the tallis suggests the time she spent with Papa, the locket, the time she spent with Mama. Those of you in that club, or who have read that book, can you talk about what *all* these objects, together, symbolize?"

Soon suggestions were flying. "It's like all those objects, they're her memories!"

I signaled for Gabe to add on. "Well-l-l-l," he said, "maybe all those things are for the people that she's thinking about. So, like, the tallis is her dad, and the locket is her mom?"

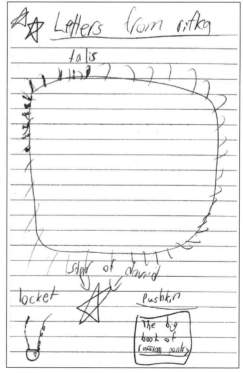

FIG. 6–1

"So you're thinking that each of those objects *symbolizes* the people she loves and misses? They're little reminders of the people she has left behind?"

"All of you, think about what the objects in your book—taken together—symbolize, as a whole. Turn and talk!"

READ ON, REMEMBERING THAT EVERYTHING IS IN THE BOOK ON PURPOSE

Readers, for homework tonight, read on in your club book. As you read, keep an eye out for lines, objects, paragraphs, parts that convey one of the themes of the story. When you find that part, think, "How does this part fit with what the story is trying to teach about life?" Reread the part of the text that you think might be symbolic and ask, "Why might the author have . . . ?" Ask about word choices, about details that are included. Remember that everything is in the book on purpose.

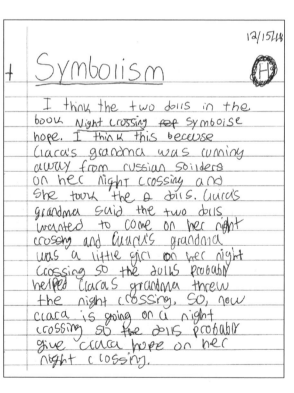

The stuff that Rifka carries with her that she got from her parents and family is almost like having family with her. It's like those things are her parents and help her remember to keep going so she can get to them.

What does the Gold Cadalac represent? 3/9
• The fight between mom and dad!??
• The fact that mother won't use the Cadalac
• She is afraid because WHITES HATE blacks having nicer things than them, that car is nice for a white man. They don't, won't, take that.
• Blacks don't get treated well in the first place.

12/15/14
+ Symbolism (H)
I think the two dolls in the book Night crossing symbolise hope. I think this becuase Clara's grandma was cuming away from russian soilders on her night crossing and she took the 2 dolls. Clara's grandma said the two dolls wanted to come on her night crossing and Clara's grandma was a little girl on her night crossing so the dolls probably helped Clara's grandma threw the night crossing. So, now Clara is going on a night crossing so the dolls probably give Clara hope on her night crossing.

FIG. 6–2

Determining Themes

I N THIS UNIT, you have helped children know that although, yes, reading is all about holding tight to the often hair-raising, death-defying dramas of historical fiction books, reading is not only about following the literal action of the story. Reading is also about coming away with deeper thoughts about what bravery or friendship is, or about how loss and defeat can be handled, or what compassion feels like. In other words, this unit aims to help young people read between the lines so they come away with bigger ideas about their lives and their world. The unit teaches readers to interpret, to determine themes.

While all good stories are really about ideas, these are rarely presented to the reader neatly arranged on a plate. This is where process comes in. When teaching writing, teachers around the world tell kids that beautiful writing isn't the result of magic, but is the product of using deliberate strategies. Children learn that they can admire the work of another writer, and then try to use similar strategies in their own writing, making their writing more closely approximate the texts they admire. In reading, too, kids need to learn that deep, accountable interpretations of a text are not the result of magic, but of strategies that can be taught and learned.

To teach kids those strategies, it is important for us as teachers and as designers of curriculum to spy on ourselves when we're engaged in the interpretive work we hope our kids will learn to do. We must take note of the specific strategies we use that pay off for us and yield insights.

This session arises from TCRWP staff members and mentor teachers studying our own reading and finding that once we have a big idea or two in our heads, we often read forward in texts—or reread—with these ideas in mind, as a way to grow those nascent ideas, revising them as we proceed. Sometimes two moments in the text that are intimately connected will be physically separated by a score of pages. We might encounter a passage that strikes a chord, and soon we are turning back to details and phrases and incidents from earlier parts of the text.

We grow those ideas until we have much larger ideas—the kind that can be applied not just to one book but to other books, to our lives, and to our world.

IN THIS SESSION, you'll remind students that when readers have developed an interpretation of a book, they keep it in mind, using it like a lens, growing and shaping that interpretation as they read on.

GETTING READY

✔ Review the "Determining Themes/Cohesion" strand in the Narrative Reading Learning Progression.

✔ Prior to this session, read aloud Chapters 6 and 7 of *Number the Stars*.

✔ Find a few examples from students who have paused in their reading to generate and jot provocative, significant ideas (see Connection).

✔ Find a book club that can share a fresh, big idea generated by their writing about reading, or plan to borrow the example we use (see Teaching).

✔ Have chart paper and marker to write this idea: "War makes children grow up early" (see Active Engagement).

✔ Provide a large Post-it or two (pink or another bright color) to each student (see Link and Homework).

✔ Make copies of "Determining Themes/Cohesion" strand in the Narrative Reading Learning Progression for students. Sending this home with students is optional (see Homework).

Determining Themes

CONNECTION

Share examples of a few readers from the class who have generated provocative, important ideas as they read.

"Readers, I've been thinking about the big ideas, the interpretations, that you and your clubs have already started to grow in this unit, and I just need to share with you some of the amazing thinking you've been doing. When the Pioneer club read *Dandelions*, a picture book about the Westward Expansion and living out on the prairie, Kobe came up with this idea" (see Figure 7–1).

"Izzy also pushed the pause button as she was reading. I watched her reading *Letters from Rifka*, and at one point she looked ready to explode with an idea. She put her idea into this entry" (see Figure 7–2).

❖ **Name the teaching point.**

"Readers, today I want to remind you that once you have paused to develop an interpretation of a book, you almost wear that idea—that interpretation—like a pair of glasses, like a lens. You can read through that lens, saying, 'Ah yes, this goes with my interpretation!' or 'Huh? This makes me think something new.'"

<table>
<tr><td>◆ COACHING</td></tr>
</table>

So often you will see kids come up with a great idea about a book, and then they seem to completely forget about that idea when they resume the next day's reading. It's as if coming up with an idea is something they do in the moment, which generates a temporary thrill. You need to teach them that holding onto an idea while reading forward in a book is essential.

You may wonder how you can teach this lesson when the Allies are not a club in your classroom. You have a few options—the best is to substitute a club that is in your classroom that has done similar work (perhaps with your coaching!). But you also can act as if the Allies were a club you worked with during an earlier year of teaching.

The dandelions are having a hard time moving from one place to another just like Bolton family.

FIG. 7–1 Kobe imbues small details with big meanings.

I think the author is trying to tell me that friends always help eachother, and they are following their heart.

FIG. 7–2 Izzy has recorded her big ideas onto Post-its.

TEACHING

Tell about some readers who developed an idea about their book (one that will later prove applicable to the read-aloud) and then put that idea aside, finding new ideas.

"Readers, I want to tell you about an idea that the Allies created. They just started reading *The House of Sixty Fathers* and they've already found passages that seemed to be written in bold. They paused to grow big ideas—and they started by thinking that the little boy in the book, Tien Pao, has to be awfully responsible considering he is such a young kid. They wanted to come up with a life lesson, with a theme for the book, so they tried saying, 'This story is teaching us that . . .' and they came up with this as a possible theme for the book: 'This story is teaching us that war makes children grow up quickly.'

"They then read on. When new ideas came up, they thought, 'Does that new idea fit with the idea I've already developed?' It is as if they looked at the rough draft of a theme (and the text they were reading) as if they were wearing their existing idea like a pair of special glasses. They looked through those special glasses thinking 'Ah, yes! This fits' or 'Hmm, . . . This makes me think something new.'"

Recruit the class to join you in seeing one club's newest idea through the lens of their original idea, helping the members of the class practice synthesizing ideas.

"Let's do this together. Pretend you are a member of the Allies club, and you came up with the idea that the book teaches readers that war makes kids grow up early." I pretended the theme was a pair of glasses, put them on, and said as an aside, "You wouldn't want to leave an idea like theirs unused! No way." Then I said, "I know you don't actually know the book, but you can still do this with me. Are you wearing the lens of that idea, that theme—war makes kids grow up early?"

The kids signaled yes. I said, "We could read more of the story now, looking through the lens of the existing idea. Kadija did that and came up with another idea from the next part of the story. It relates to a pig that has become Tien Pao's friend. Let's look at Kadija's idea through the lens of the idea that war makes children grow up quickly." Kadija stood beside me and read aloud:

The House of Sixty Fathers

I think that the pig is kind of like a human to him. It's kind of like he is a pet that can be his companion. Since he is all alone, he is feeding it since it is like a pet. He tries to control him and he punishes him. I think that if his parents were there it would be different because there would be someone else to punish the pig.

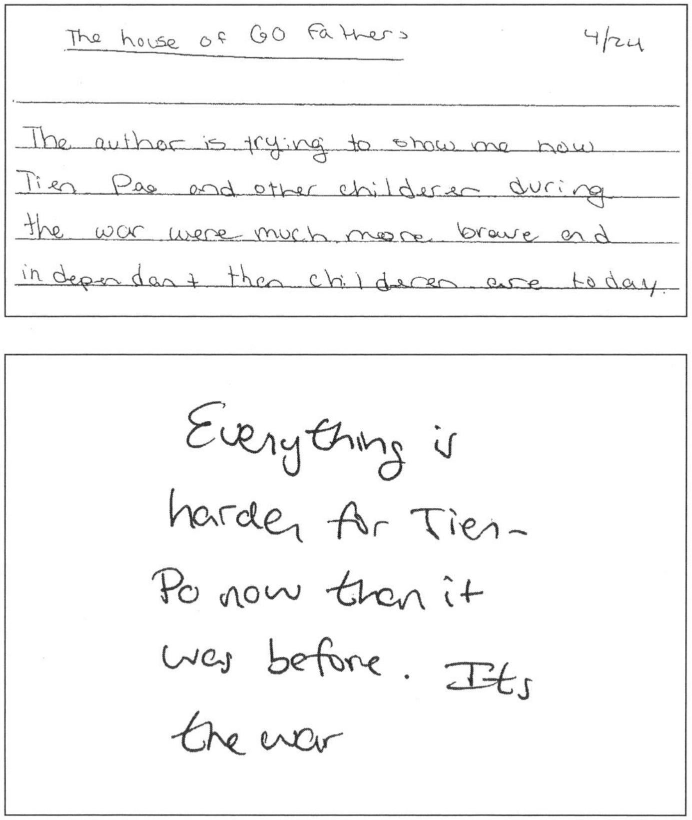

It is important for kids to realize that the Allies created the idea that war makes kids grow up. The book does not come straight out and say that.

This concept—reading on in a book, taking one person's tentative theory as a lens through which you see upcoming sections of the text—is critical. Act out that you literally put on a pair of glasses that let you see through the lens of one idea. Here, you put on the lens of the idea that war makes kids grow up early. Then you read on with that lens as if it were a pair of glasses, looking for evidence that supports or informs this idea.

The house of 60 Fathers   4/24

The author is trying to show me how Tien Pao and other childeren during the war were much more brave and independant then childeren are today.

Everything is harder for Tien-Po now then it was before. Its the war

FIG. 7–3

The House of Sixty Fathers

I think that the pig is kind of like a human to him. It's kind of like he is a pet that can be his companion. Since he is all alone he is feeding it since it is like a pet. He tries to controll him & he punishes him. I think that if his parents were there it would be different because there would be someone else to punish the pig. Also, the pig is the only living thing in his life other than the ducklings witch are kind of like the things that he has fun taking care of. It seems that it is important to socialize. So he, since there aren't any humans will even socialize with farm animals. Now I think that he is lonely, and animals comfort him and make him not as boared. He was able to play games with them wich is pretty cool.

FIG. 7–4

"Kadija is now saying that if Tien Pao's parents were with him, someone else could punish his pig and he wouldn't have to do it. What do you think? Does this fit with the existing idea? Is it an example of the larger life message that war makes kids grow up too quickly? Does it extend that idea, change it a bit? Or is this altogether separate? Turn and talk."

After a minute, I convened the class and asked Kadija what she thought. Triumphant, Kadija said, "The ideas go together! Because war has made Tien Pao grow up early, acting like an adult when he is still a kid. He has to tell the pig how to behave."

"Yeah, he has to act like a parent because his parents aren't there," added Brandon.

You will notice that you are using big idea and theme as if they were interchangeable. That's okay. The truth is that the big ideas that kids are generating now are rough-draft efforts at a theme.

Name the work this child is doing that you hope others can do, in other texts. In this case, point out that the original idea can be the lens through which the reader can read the text and make new ideas.

"So what I'm hearing is this: You created an idea out of Chapter 1—that war makes kids grow up early—and in Chapter 2, you have an example of that idea. Good work! You developed a theme and then read on, seeing the new text through the lens of that idea. And look at how your idea has developed!"

ACTIVE ENGAGEMENT

Scaffold children as they practice viewing texts through the lens of an interpretation. Ask your students to put on the lens of an interpretation one club developed, applying that to the read-aloud book (if it is applicable).

"So before we move on, I'm going to ask you to try something a little unexpected. Pretend that the Allies' idea (that war makes children grow up early) is an idea *your* club came up with when reading the early chapters of *Number the Stars*." I jotted this idea up on chart paper to help them remember it:

War makes children grow up early.

"Again, put on the idea, 'War makes children grow up early.'" I slid on the idea as if it were a pair of glasses. "Now let's look back to the part of *Number the Stars* that we heard earlier in which the soldiers bang on the door at night, saying 'Let us in,' and they search for Ellen and her family. Recall how Annemarie reached for the necklace around her friend's neck. 'Hold still,' she said, and yanked it off. Remember how she held that Star of David necklace pressed into her hand as the soldiers interrogated her.

"Remember, you are seeing this text through the lens of 'Children grow up early during times of war.' When we read that passage earlier, we all thought, 'Annemarie's brave.' So now, tell each other what comes to mind as you look *now* through the lens of the theme that war makes children grow up before their time. Turn and talk."

As the children talked, I crouched alongside them and listened in. After a bit, I reconvened the class to crystallize what I'd heard: "I heard you say so many smart things—like many of you said that kids have to grow up during war because grown-ups can't protect children like Annemarie from having to act in grown-up and brave ways. Or you said that war makes kids grow up fast because they have to make life-and-death decisions. I love that you added the word *because* to the initial theme, and developed it more. That's how readers grow their thinking."

A word of advice: As some children gather up parts of the story to support their ideas, they will ignore all the parts of the story that don't support that idea. Don't fret about this right now. We'll address that in the next session. Keep in mind that as children add a new reading practice, they'll often run with it, sometimes seeming to have forgotten all the other work they've done as readers so far. It's okay; their enthusiasm is actually a good force.

It may seem like an amazing coincidence that the idea children had developed for their book, The House of Sixty Fathers, *is applicable also to* Number the Stars, *but in fact, you'll come to see later that many big ideas are broadly applicable. You'll find the idea is pertinent to a fair number of their books—certainly to* Letters from Rifka, *for example. You'll find that the themes they are identifying in their books probably pertain to other books as well—hence the label "universal themes." A word of caution: Don't point this out to children yet, because this will be one of the special realizations that provide new energy toward the end of this unit.*

There will be lots of instances like this one where you are called upon to paraphrase what you've just heard a child or two say. You'll "round up," but don't replace what the children said with what you wish they had said. As you help them learn to interpret, keep in mind that you have a lot more teaching to do, and that teaching will lead them to revisit their interpretations, ratcheting these up bit by bit.

LINK

Recap what you hope readers have learned that is transferable to other texts.

"So readers, always remember that after you have paused to grow big ideas about texts, when you read on, if your book continues to give off lots of ideas, one of your jobs will be to examine those new ideas through the lens of your initial idea. That initial idea will change. Perhaps you'll add a *'because . . .'* statement to your idea, or perhaps you'll make that idea more precise or broader.

"Do you remember that earlier we talked about how stories unfurl along a plot timeline and a history timeline?" Children nodded. "Well, today you learned that your *ideas* about a book also develop in ways that can be timelined. Before you get started reading, look back on your jottings and think, 'What big idea or two am I carrying forward as I read?' I've put a brilliant pink Post-it on each of your reading spots. Write your most current draft of a theme about your club book on that Post-it, and leave it out where you and I can see it. Then read on. And I'll leave some extra pink Post-its because I'm pretty sure your idea might change as you keep reading on."

This big Post-it will become central to the ongoing unit, so I encourage you to actually do this. Of course, it need not be pink!

Be Informed by the Learning Progressions

IF YOU KEEP IN MIND YOUR LEARNING PROGRESSIONS, this can help you confer and lead small groups. Note the level of work done by a child or a cluster of children, and then think, "What's next?" and teach toward that goal.

Remind readers to use the "Inferring about Characters" strand of the learning progression.

As you confer and lead small groups today, you'll want to remind readers to keep strands of the learning progression in front of them as they work. Those strands decentralize your teaching, allowing children to work to ramp up their comprehension even when you are not at their elbows. Children who need to be reminded of work with character traits and changes can note when they talk in overly simplified ways about a character. Remind them that in fourth grade, they need to account for the complexity of characters. Kirsti is not just happy, nor is Annemarie only kind. Kirsti is also childish or naïve or unaware. You can give students practice at thinking about characters using precise terms by asking them to shift from their club book to *Number the Stars* for a minute. "Take Kirsti. What *exactly* is she like?" You can give students miniature word walls to help them internalize the work of taking a millisecond to think, "Wait. I don't want to use just any word. What is the precisely true word?" You can remind readers that often it helps to use lots of words to say what you mean, not just one. Again, if you use *Number the Stars* as your example, you could say: "Kirsti is always cheerful even when the world around her is full of depressing things and her sister and her parents leave her out of matters." Of course, the important thing will be to channel readers to do similar thinking with the characters from their historical fiction books.

The learning progression will nudge readers beyond characterizing people with more precise terms to new horizons. The progression will remind them that characters are different in different settings, in different relationships. You might channel students to think about characters using language such as "Sometimes my character is . . . For example . . . But other times my character is . . . For example. . . ." Alternatively, you could coach them to use language such as "My character has different sides to him

(or her). On the outside . . . But on the inside. . . ." Or, "In the beginning, I thought my character was . . . But now I am realizing that deep down, my character is. . . ."

Using the "Determining Themes/Cohesion" strand of the learning progression.

Your students' work with characters and their life lessons and changes will often be the avenue to them growing tentative ideas about a story's theme. As the "Determining Themes/Cohesion" strand of the learning progression suggests, you'll want them to think about the possible themes early on in their reading, and be testing these ideas out as they read on, something you have now taught the class to do. Remind them to "put on the lens of a theme," and to read on in a story, letting the upcoming events support or alter their ideas.

If the reader thinks first about what the main character is learning, that can lead to a first draft of a theme. Rifka learns that even when she is alone, she can make a life for herself—and the child reading *Letters from Rifka* will say, "The theme of this book might be that Rifka learns that even when she is alone and in a place she doesn't know, she can make a life for herself." Help these readers read on and find several instances in the text that support or alter that theme. Point out that the "Determining Themes/Cohesion" strand of the learning progression can offer them tips. They'll note that it suggests they especially look for places in the novel where the character makes a decision or realizes something big. Nudge students to use that tip—gleaned from the tool itself—to help them read interpretively. When children later meet to talk, suggest they put a Post-it containing their big idea on the desk as they read on, and later put it in the center of a club meeting as an artifact, as described in the following share. Some clubs make a "conversation board" that contains a blank space at the center for children to put the Post-it that is in play in a book club discussion.

Eventually you will want to help students reword the theme so it is more broadly applicable. The prompt "This is important because . . ." can help. You can also tell the

(continues)

MID-WORKSHOP TEACHING
Readers Enlarge Their Interpretations about Texts

"I want to teach you a few ways to make sure that your big ideas are really big. Developing a big idea or a theme takes time, just as it did when you were developing a thesis for the essay in writing workshop. Here are some hints.

"A theme can be said in one word—or in a few sentences. Grace started work on her themes in *Letters from Rifka* by writing 'homesickness' on her pink Post-it—and it is true that Rifka is homesick in this story. But it is important to be able to talk about the theme of a story as a sentence, and not just as a word. When Brandon read *The House of Sixty Fathers*, he may have started with 'growing up.' But he went on to think, 'What is this book teaching about war?' and 'What is this book teaching about growing up?' and that is how he came up with the theme, 'War makes kids grow up fast.' So push yourself to be able to name the theme of your book in a sentence or two.

"My other tip is this. Themes or big ideas have more power when you think of them as claims about the world, rather than just about the book. If you can use words like *kids* or *people* rather than specific characters' names, it helps you see how an idea applies to other characters. So, Brandon's claim was first, 'War makes Tien Pao grow up fast,' and then becomes, 'War makes kids grow up too fast.'

"So, everyone, you have some more time to read. As you read on, be making sure that you can say the theme of your story in a sentence or two. Write that sentence onto your big pink Post-it."

student, "Try deleting the character's name, so that instead of saying, 'Rifka learns . . .' you say, 'Readers learn that in life. . . .'"

When your students meet in their clubs to talk today, you can listen to club conversations to see whether kids "take up" one another's claims and insights and think about the text, along with their own ideas, through the lens of one another's ideas.

Help them to do this. You may want to begin by transcribing their conversations and noting the great ideas that are mentioned and then left by the roadside. Then you could intervene, saying something like "I'm listening closely to your conversation, and I hear you talking about patterns in actions, reasons for actions. Those are ways to dig under the plot, so nicely done! But I want to point out that when you're in a book talk, you need to take up one another's ideas. Remember when I said that you can read a book through the lens of an idea, like the lens of Kadija's idea that war makes people grow up fast? Right now, I'm hearing too many amazing ideas that are just left at the side of the road." To make your point, you might reread a transcript of their conversation, asking them to raise a finger every time a new idea was brought up and count them. "Now, I suggest you go back and use some of these ideas as a lens to examine the text and help grow your themes."

Readers Note Different Ideas that Fit under the Tent of a Theme

Convene the class and tell the students about a club that thought across the big ideas individual members were pursuing, generating an overarching club idea.

"Readers, can you come to the meeting area and bring your books and pink Post-its?" I waited until the children had all settled down. "Let me tell you about what another club did with their ideas and see if you are game for doing something similar. This club met around a big sheet of construction paper. The kids first laid out their pink Post-its (their big ideas about the book they were reading), like so." I laid out four giant-sized pink Post-its on the chart paper, hanging from the easel.

> The father isn't the way he used to be because he used to like to play the fiddle and make music, but he changed after the death of Anna and Caleb's mother. He became more serious.

> Anna is resistant to Sarah's mothering her because she is used to her real mother.

> Caleb is getting close to Sarah but feels Anna doesn't want that.

> Sarah misses home, but she is learning bit by bit to care for this new family.

"They'd been reading *Sarah, Plain and Tall*, like our Pioneers did earlier." Most students knew this book, so I summarized just briefly. "It is the story of a father and his two children, Anna and Caleb, who lived during the time of Westward

Expansion in a rural area with vast stretches of farmland. The children's mother had died before the story began." I went on to explain how the father had found a bride in a special catalog and how Sarah had traveled far to live with this family and decide about marrying the father and becoming part of the family.

Turning to their pink Post-its, I said, "My challenge to this club—and to each of your clubs—is this: Can you think across all the ideas you've brought to the table (I gestured to all the Post-its I'd laid out) and try to grow one or two huge, important ideas?" I pointed to the collection of ideas about *Sarah, Plain and Tall*. "This is hard intellectual work, so turn your brains on full power."

After a bit, I stopped the buzz of talk and shared some ideas I'd heard—how *everyone* in the family had to decide if things were going to work out, not just Sarah, or how you can't just order a new family out of a catalog. After a club grew a big tent idea—that *Sarah, Plain and Tall* shows how different people deal with loss, I asked the club members to find supporting evidence in the text and they pointed out that Anna didn't want someone new to fill the hole from her first mother. And that Sarah is homesick for her lost home. The dad didn't play music because he misses his first wife. Stopping all the clubs in the midst of their conversation about the *Sarah, Plain and Tall* Post-its, I shared what the one club had discovered.

I then encouraged all of clubs to review their own pink Post-its in a similar way, working to figure out big tent ideas of their own.

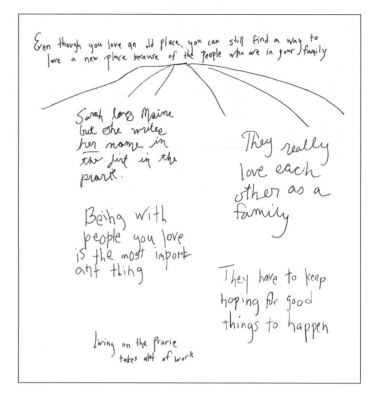

Even though you love an old place, you can still find a way to love a new place because of the people who are in your family

Sarah loves Maine but she writes her name in the dirt in the prarie.

Being with people you love is the most important thing

They really love each other as a family

They have to keep hoping for good things to happen

living on the prarie takes alot of work

FIG. 7–5   This is the theory chart that the Pioneers created, to bring their pink Post-its together under one overarching idea.

DEVELOP A BIG TENT IDEA ON YOUR OWN

Readers, you'll want to practice reading your novels thinking about themes, about big tent ideas. If your club already did this work today with your club book, see if you can read on with that idea as a lens through which you can see the story. You could also try this work with any book you've read recently.

As you read on in your book, try to grow more big ideas, to find more themes. By next year, readers will be expected to find several themes in a novel, so there are more themes in your book. Jot big-idea Post-its as you read and then, after you read for half an hour or so, arrange those Post-its in front of you. Study those Post-its and try to see connections among them and among any earlier work your club has done around themes in this book. One way or another, think of a big tent idea that covers most of the smaller ideas you have about the book. You may have more than one big tent idea, so jot them down in your reading notebook.

Pause to clear your brain, and then look at your big tent idea(s) again. Ask yourself, "Does this big tent really work?" Does it communicate what's important about the smaller ideas? Do you need to revise the big tent idea to make it clearer?

It may help you to see examples of big tent ideas for books you may know:

Skylark (the sequel to *Sarah, Plain and Tall*): Even if you love an old place, you can still find a way to love a new place because of the people who are in your family.

Maggie's Door: As people move to new places, they hold onto things that remind them of their old home and the people they love.

Then read on, viewing the text through the lens of that idea. Be sure to keep your "Determining Themes" learning progression at your side and work to make your thinking and writing *at least* fourth-grade level!

Narrative Reading Learning Progression		
Grade 3	Grade 4	Grade 5
INTERPRETIVE READING		

Determining Themes/Cohesion

Grade 3: At the end of a story, I can say a few sentences about the big life lesson (the theme) that a character has learned.

Grade 4: I read, asking, "What's this story really about?" and I come up with tentative ideas that I test as I read on. I have an internalized checklist of what makes a good interpretation—that the theme applies to most of the story, that it suggests a life lesson. I know that often the theme becomes most clear at the end, but then I can look back and see the theme trace through other parts, such as times when a character makes a decision or realizes something big.

Grade 5: I read, asking, "What seem to be the big themes of this story?" I can figure out a couple of themes that are especially significant, noting which are best supported. To think about these, I tie together what several significant parts of the story seem to mean. I know themes are shown not only by the content of the text, but also in the way it is written.

Supporting Thinking with Text Evidence

Grade 3: I can talk and write about parts of the story that support my thinking.

Grade 4: After deciding on a theme that is important to a story, I can look back on the story, finding textual details from across the text that support that theme.

Grade 5: I can cite details that support each of several themes, keeping straight which details support which themes. I don't just summarize—I also sometimes quote. I know the exact words used can help convey the theme.

Deepening Interpretation through Collaboration and Close Reading

IN THIS SESSION, you'll teach your students that readers are open to new ideas, both as they read and in conversation with other readers, and they can use these ideas to make their interpretations more powerful.

GETTING READY

✔ Prior to this session, read aloud Chapter 8 of *Number the Stars*.

✔ Prepare to tell students about a time when you interpreted what a text was about, found support for that interpretation, and then revised your initial idea. You may use the example provided or your own example of a text and interpretation work (see Connection and Teaching).

✔ Be prepared to read aloud and perhaps display an excerpt from Chapter 6 from *Number the Stars*, possibly using a document camera (see Active Engagement).

✔ Be prepared to find a club that will converse in front of the others, fishbowl style, and be ready to coach club members to stay with each other's ideas (see Active Engagement).

✔ Display the "Growing Powerful Book Club Conversations" chart (see Active Engagement).

✔ Display the "Readers of Historical Fiction . . ." anchor chart (see Link).

✔ Your readers will benefit from having strands of the learning progressions on hand as they work, and especially the "Determining Themes" strand (see Mid-Workshop Teaching).

✔ Provide the "Thought Prompts for Generating Quick Writes" chart to help students generate quick writes about their reading (see Share and Homework).

IN THIS SESSION, you'll build on the past few sessions, encouraging students to develop richer interpretations through collaboration and close reading. You'll be putting conversation at the heart of interpretation, teaching students that by talking together about a text, they come to see more in it, and their ideas become stronger and more accountable. Your hope is that this session not only encourages students to *revise* their initial interpretations, it also encourages them to entertain alternate perspectives and to adapt their ideas to the ideas of others.

Often you will find that your teaching feels as if it is moving from one side of the boat to another. You teach kids to use exclamation points—and then you teach them to be sparing in their use of exclamation points. Earlier in this unit, you taught students to become committed to a big idea—to a theme—and to look at the upcoming portions of a book through the lens of that interpretation. In this session, you go to the other side of the boat, encouraging children to maintain their wide-open receptivity to new ideas.

The session was originally developed because we found that once we rallied students around the importance of growing interpretations of a text, they tended to hold so doggedly to their interpretations that their thinking stalled—and sometimes they would ignore parts of the story that didn't fit their interpretation. They seemed to think the purpose of a discussion was to defend rather than to develop ideas. We began, therefore, asking students to talk about how their thinking was changed during a discussion. And if the child said, "My ideas are the same. I was right," we expressed sympathy, consoling the child by saying, "Oh, well, too bad. Maybe next time you'll have one of those great conversations where your mind is on fire with new thinking."

You will also want to address head-on the idea that deep thinkers are people whose ideas are changed through conversation. This session aims to do that, readjusting children's stances and posture, coaching them into an attitude of receptivity.

Deepening Interpretation through Collaboration and Close Reading

CONNECTION

Introduce children to the idea of *a journey of thought*, in which one idea leads to the next.

"Readers, I love to go on journeys. And I'm not talking about journeys to new places. I'm talking about journeys of thought. I absolutely love to have one idea—a really good one, that I'm excited about—and then to find that the one idea allows me to see further than I've seen before, so I end up having another idea—an even better one. And then sometimes *that* idea lets me see even further, so I keep going and going, with one idea leading to the next. That's what I call a *journey of thought*.

"Sometimes that journey is even better, even richer, if you take it with other people, discussing and growing ideas together."

❖ **Name the teaching point.**

"Today I want to teach you that in a good book, as in a good conversation, you can feel your thinking being changed. When you are open to new thinking as you read and as you discuss ideas with other readers, you can build richer, more powerful interpretations."

TEACHING

Tell children about a journey of thought you had with a friend, and how it led you to a new idea—and a new lens through which to read on.

"Let me show you what I mean. When I read Chapter 6 of *Number the Stars*, I was struck by the part where Mama remembers her dog, Trofast, so vividly, how he waited for her every afternoon in the same spot on the path, his tail wagging. That scene is important because it shows Mama never forgets anyone she cares about. She doesn't forget her Aunt Gitte and her wonderful flowers, and her best childhood friend, Helena. Even though she doesn't talk about Annemarie's sister, Lise, she must remember every detail about her.

"But then, a friend who recently read this book brought out another idea, saying the dog is important because his name Trofast means *faithful*, and that's how Annemarie and her mother are being to Ellen—faithful. They're sticking by her

Often across the year and across the curriculum, you will teach—or remind—students to use prompts that support them in going on a journey of thought. When students write essays, when they talk about texts during read-aloud, even earlier in this unit when they begin to use extended writing as a way to prepare for their club conversations, prompts such as "I used to think . . . , but now I realize . . ." and "When I first read this I thought . . . , but now, after rereading it, I realize . . ." act as scaffolds to help children progress from one thought to another, to learn this sort of flexibility of thinking.

The work you are doing here helps support the "Determining Themes" strand of the learning progression, and it also helps students to do the analytic reading that some high-stakes standards are asking them to do. In this instance, you've taken a part of the text and asked, "How might this one part of the story be important to the whole story?" Your analysis of part in relation to whole is specific here and supports the work on the learning progression as well.

just like Trofast stuck by Mama when she was a girl. My friend and I talked more about this idea of being faithful. We started to think that the idea of being faithful isn't just about one or two characters, it's something important in the story. After talking some more, we decided that *Number the Stars* might be about the importance of being faithful and taking care of people you care about.

"Later on, I reread bits of the book with this idea, this lens of being faithful to family and friends. I found this bit in Chapter 3, when the family is discussing the closure of Mrs. Hirsch's button shop and their worries about her family. Mama tries to reassure the girls saying, 'Friends will take care of them . . . That's what friends do.' I think this might be a really important idea in this book. Now when I read the rest of the story, I'll keep using that idea as a lens: being faithful to those you care about. I'll also want to keep discussing this idea with other readers to get their thoughts and to keep growing the idea—and maybe get some brand-new ideas that I haven't even thought of yet."

ACTIVE ENGAGEMENT

Explain that it is important to be willing to listen to the ideas of others and to use those ideas instead of your own. Set children up to carry someone else's idea with them as they read on in the class novel.

"Readers, it's easy to hold tight to an idea, especially one you're proud of. But you can learn so much more by being willing to outgrow your own best ideas. One way to do that is to be in conversations with others who think differently than you do. You just heard about my journey of thought with *Number the Stars*. When I opened myself up to new thinking, I found my way to a deeper interpretation. You can, too.

"Let's try this," I said. "Pretend that your club just talked about Chapter 6 of *Number the Stars* and one club member really pushed the idea that this whole book seems to be developing the themes that friends take care of friends, and that is it important to be faithful to those you care about." Then I displayed a small excerpt I'd chosen from later in that chapter and said, "Pretend you are reading on in the book, but you don't just leave your friend's idea by the side of the road. Carry it with you." Then I explained that instead of them actually reading on, I'd read aloud a bit more of the chapter and I did, reminding them to listen with the idea "How does this fit with or extend the idea that one possible theme for *Number the Stars* is 'Friends take care of each other'?" I added, "Be sure you let your thinking move to new places. Be sure you let the book change your initial idea."

After I read, the clubs talked, and I coached into their conversations, saying things like, "Practice having a conversation being open to changing your mind. Let something feel important that messes up your initial theory." As children talked, I voiced over, "Remember to ask why. Like, what seems to be of concern to Annemarie's parents? Why are they seeming to talk in code?"

Locate one club that might be willing to fishbowl their conversation in front of the class. As they talked about the class novel, I encouraged them to build off of and extend each other's ideas.

I listened in as children tried this work, and took note of one club whose collaboration was evident—the kids had pulled in close enough to make eye contact and were listening to one another—but whose conversation would benefit from coaching. I asked this club to reenact their conversation.

You'll want to be ready to spotlight a club of kids who have great ideas but tend to jump from one idea to the next. You'll be encouraging them to stay with and extend each other's ideas.

After a minute, I reconvened the class. "Civil War Book Club, will you join me?" I waited until all four kids in the club were seated by me at the front of the meeting area, then said, "I want us to try something a little different right now. Will the rest of you watch closely as the Civil War Club reenacts the conversation they just had? I'm going to be coaching in. Pay attention to the suggestions I make and to how this group responds. Gabe, remind kids if they need reminders about what they said, earlier.

"Max, will you start us off?" I said, and gestured to him.

"Annemarie's dad talked about skipping school as a 'vacation.' That was a secret code so the girls wouldn't get scared," Max said. "But as we kept reading, I heard words like *safety* and *dangerous*. So, umm, maybe the parents *wanted* the girls to know that something serious was happening?"

Gabe poked Tyrell, who responded, "You're right, it did seem strange that the parents wanted the girls to take a 'vacation' from school. Were they trying to keep the girls from being worried? But, the parents still talked about safety and danger. I wonder if they miss the dead sister when they are on vacation."

I looked up at the kids on the rug, said, "Watch now," then coached in. "At first, Tyrell, your response showed you were listening to Max—you talked about the idea he brought up about parents talking in code. But then you seemed to jump to a whole different idea when you mentioned that perhaps the family gets lonely for Lise when they are on vacation. Any chance you could think longer off of Max's idea about talking in code, calling something a vacation, which clearly wasn't?"

Tyrell said, "Umm, okay. Umm . . . I'm interested in why Annemarie's parents called it a vacation when it wasn't but they still wanted the girls to know *something* about what was happening. Why would they want that?"

Debrief what just happened, then ask students to turn and talk about what else made this conversation a productive, collaborative one. Remind them to carry these ideas into their own book talks.

I gave Tyrell a thumbs up and the group talked with energy about his question. Pausing the fishbowl, I said to the whole class, "Did you see how the tone of the conversation changed once Tyrell opened himself up to new thinking? He was actually wondering as he spoke—why would the parents do two things that seemed to conflict with each other? They pretend they're taking the girls on a vacation, yet they talk ominously about safety and danger. What else did you notice about their conversation?"

The children talked and then after thirty seconds, I shared out some of the class's observations: that Tyrell asking a question of Max led the club to grow its thinking, and that certain phrases, like "I'm interested in . . ." and "Why would . . . ?" ignited deeper thinking.

Then I said, "Remember this strategy when you are discussing books. Try to use words and questions to bring out more thinking and to connect ideas. This way, your conversation—and your thinking—can grow. Throughout this unit, we have been saying that for a club to go well, members need to really listen to one another. To do that, it helps to build

You may decide to skip this invitation for a club conversation, based on time. But look ahead because the link is lovely and requires that clubs have a chance to talk.

from what one another says, not start on a new journey of thought every time a new person speaks. I'm going to ask you to make a renewed commitment to doing just that."

For a minute or two, the clubs talked.

LINK

Freeze the class and ask them to look at their body postures, to note what the conversations look and feel like, and to draw on this image often in the future.

After a few minutes, I said, in a stage whisper, "Readers, freeze just where you are. I don't want to mess up a bit of this. It is so beautiful. Right now, without turning your heads, shift just your eyes a tiny bit so you see what this room looks like. It is so beautiful. And the ways you have started talking to each other is beautiful, too—so collaborative. Remember this sort of listening, this sort of talking, this sort of positioning when you are in our clubs, which won't be until tomorrow. It's this kind of intense respect and interest that you'll need to grow ideas together.

"Depending on how far you are in your club's book—I know a few of you just started a book today—many of you entered today's conversation with a theme in mind for your book. I'm pretty sure that you've already started to add to that idea or to make another idea or to change your idea. It is time now to shift to reading, and you won't be in a club today. When you read, read the way you've been listening, really listening to the text, expecting to go on a journey of thought.

"Before you head off to reading, will you look over the anchor chart and think about the work you are going to be trying to do especially today? When you know what your work will be, give me a thumbs-up signal and then you can get started."

You may need to be ready to coach the child into how he or she can stay with an idea that is "on the table." Almost always, it will be helpful if a child asks a question such as "Why do you think . . . ?" or "How does that go with . . . ?"

Sometimes, just calling attention to posture will make everyone sit up a bit taller. If almost all of your students are demonstrating wonderful listening postures, go ahead and tell them to look around. If, on the other hand, you find that most groups have devolved into a kind of messy, distracted posture, then only ask those groups to freeze who are demonstrating what you are trying to teach, asking the others to look at those particular clubs for ideas for their own clubs.

Teach Readers to Pay Attention to Tone and Mood

THE CONCEPT OF A JOURNEY of thought is an important one in this curriculum. After all, consider the shape of each unit of study. The bends in the road of a unit signal that the units, themselves, are designed to support journeys of thought. In this unit, you began by supporting students at actually "getting" the more complex texts they are now reading, and you have moved toward supporting interpretation. To do that, you taught students to pause to think, "What's this book really about?" and then to sustain their thinking about an interpretation across time and more recently, to be open to new ideas and new insights about an existing idea.

As always, you will want to confer into students' reading, keeping track of their goals and their reading work. Pay attention especially to students' volume of reading, making sure that by now they are well into their second or third book. If they aren't, then too much time is being spent talking, too little writing, or children need to renew their commitment to logging the volume of reading they do at home and school. We'll assume, however, that you already have a repertoire of skills in place for helping readers to read with stamina, volume, fluency, with an interest in vocabulary, envisioning and predicting as they read.

On this particular day, even though the class wasn't working in book clubs, I asked members of the Pioneers club to meet so that I could catch up on their thinking. They had read the *Sarah, Plain and Tall* trilogy. Earlier, they had done some performance work with selected scenes and had improved their fluency. They'd worked with the "Fluency" strand of the learning progression trying to make sure their voices reflected what's going on in the story—the character's thoughts, feelings, and responses. Today, they began discussing *Caleb's Story*, the trilogy's final book. They thought the moment when the father, Papa, suddenly meets his father, who'd been absent for years, was a showstopper.

Brianna said, "When Papa says, 'This is my father. This is John Witting!' It was like boom!"

Lily agreed, "It's like a huge weight dropping down."

Malik chimed in. "I can't imagine seeing my dad after so many years, and then finding out he was alive after I thought he was dead."

Jasmine said, "Well, I think the mood gets bad or heavy, you know, because Papa is so upset about his dad coming home." Thinking aloud, she continued, "Papa's voice kind of changes, and it kind of scares everyone a little."

(continues)

MID-WORKSHOP TEACHING
Readers Keep Up Their Reading Pace

"Readers, can I have your eyes?" I waited. "We're not going to meet in clubs today, because some of you have been doing so much talking and writing that you're inching through your books. I know I've emphasized pausing to think, but a pause is a little stop in the midst of forward movement. Look, for example, at how many pages you've read so far today. You've been reading for fifteen minutes, so you should have read at least twelve pages so far. If you haven't read that much, pick up your pace.

"You're going to have twenty more minutes to read, so put a Post-it or a bookmark at fifteen pages ahead in your book and see if you can step up your speed, get lost in the story, and read, read, read. I know you're thinking as you read. You have your draft of a theme for this book. Keep the "Determining Themes" strand of the learning progression out as you read, and work on making sure your thinking is at least fourth-grade level. Get back to your reading."

Others added that even Seal, the cat, was startled by Papa's voice and ran up the stairs.

"Well, it wasn't bad the whole time. I did think that part of the scene was bad when Papa got so upset. But before that, it was. . . ." Malik stopped, trying to find the precise word. I was impressed that he was aiming for noticing more fine-grained elements of the story's tone.

The students paused, and I made a suggestion. "It sounds like you are saying that the scene started out with one kind of tone and then it changed. Is that it?"

Jumping in, Jasmine added, "Yeah, it started mysterious because he doesn't tell them about these pills. It's like he's hiding something. And he doesn't say who he is or where his home is."

"Like he's keeping a secret or something," Brianna said.

"That does sound pretty mysterious in the beginning. But you don't think it's mysterious the whole time?" I asked.

"Um, I don't think so. Because then Cassie comes in, and she is funny, and then everyone is happy to see Papa when he comes home," Lily said.

"So the mood kind of brightens, because of Cassie's arrival," I reiterated.

"Yeah. But, it's still a little mysterious because Papa's dad is still there," Jasmine said. She added, "I agree with what Lily wrote," gesturing to Lily's Post-it.

At that point, I felt I had enough information to be helpful. As usual, I began with a compliment. "Hmm, . . . I love that you are seeing that scenes aren't always just one way. You have been doing such great work paying attention to the way scenes sound and feel and rereading them together dramatically. So it makes sense now that you are coming to think about how a single scene can progress from one mood to another. I'm impressed that you are noticing tone, and mood, and paying attention to hints that the tone is changing, not just to the full-out changes.

"Remember before, when I suggested that sometimes it helps to put one thing in the middle of a conversation and to talk off that one thing? It seems to me you could put that specific passage in the middle of your conversation. You'd want to reread it aloud to each other, like you did earlier, continuing to work on the "Fluency" strand of the learning progression. You could then annotate the passage, and I find it helps to first do this individually, and then to talk with the book open, actually turning to lines from the text. It's almost like you'd be figuring out the kind of music that you hear in the beginning of this scene, in the middle, and as the scene *crescendos*, or increases in intensity, when Papa realizes his father is standing there in front of him after all these years."

The kids seemed excited. One of them suggested that the club members reread the chapter, paying attention especially to the changing tone and mood.

I nodded, saying, "Be ready to think about what kind of 'music' you are hearing." As I moved on, I noticed the chapter begins, "The morning was bright and clear when I woke, no snow or wind. I could smell coffee." It seemed likely that the chapter would progress through some very different moods.

Readers Write Fast and Furious to Continue Their Journeys of Thought

Ask children to do a quick write, using thought prompts to generate writing that will take them on a journey of thought.

"Readers, we have just three more minutes before reading time is over. In these three minutes, I'm going to ask you to write about how your thinking is changing. Start with the idea that you and your club developed during yesterday's share session or the new version you have drafted of it since then. For some of you it was 'As people move to new places, they hold onto things that remind them of their old homes and the people they love.' For some it was 'Even though you love an old place, you can still find a way to love a new place because of the people who are in your new family,' and for another group it was 'Even in the face of destruction, it's possible to have hope and find beauty.' Write about your club's idea (or about whatever idea you have had about your club book), and then about whatever your new thinking you can develop on that idea. To get you going, try using one of these thought prompts from the 'Thought Prompts for Generating Quick Writes' chart.

"So your writing might start like this":

<u>When I first read this, I thought</u> it was a story about a girl who has to travel to America by <u>herself. But I have now</u> come to realize that she isn't by herself, because all along the way, Rifka gets into relationships with other people. It is almost like she makes a substitute family.

I gestured to the chart "Thought Prompts for Generating Quick Writes" and said, "Glance at this chart and decide which of these thought prompts you will try out." After a minute, I said, "Think about how your writing will start. When I say 'Go,' start to write. I'm going to do this too. We are all going to write fast and furious, not letting our pens stop, so we fill an entire page and go on to the next page. If you finish what you are saying using one of these prompts, you can take another and keep writing. You only have three minutes, but I challenge you to try to fill the whole page, and more, in that time. Ready? . . . Go!"

The room was filled with the scratching of pens. After three minutes, I said, "Readers, it's time to stop. I want you to notice how much you all wrote. Hold your writing up so we can all see the sheer length of it.

"Readers, one reason I did this today was to show you that writing needn't take up half of reading time. In three minutes of writing, you can put tons of ideas onto the page. As you go forward, continue to be protective of your reading

---

Thought Prompts for Generating Quick Writes

- I used to think..., but now I realize....

- When I first read this, I thought..., but now, rereading it, I realize....

- On the surface, this is the story of.... But I think it is really a story about....

- Some people think this is a story about.... But I think it is really a story about....

- My ideas about...are complicated. In a way I think..., but on the other hand, I also think....

time, making sure you are reading at least forty pages a day, and remember that you can *also* write fast and furious to get lots of your thinking on paper, to help you change your ideas."

 STAY OPEN TO NEW IDEAS AS YOU READ

Readers, tonight you should devote a good amount of time to read your own books. Strive to reach your reading volume goal. At the same time, as you read, keep asking yourself, "What is the book *really* about?" Remember to stay open to new ideas as you read, as you did in class. Even if these ideas may not seem connected to your interpretation of the story, take note of them. These new ideas may take you on a journey of thought in ways that will surprise you. These ideas may inspire you to change your mind about your interpretation, perhaps more than once.

Leave a little time at the end of your homework time to do a quick write. Choose one of the thought prompts, and then go! Write fast and furious. Fill an entire page and then another. Three minutes and you're done!

Now read your quick write and circle your best thoughts. Then use those thoughts to add to or change your interpretation.

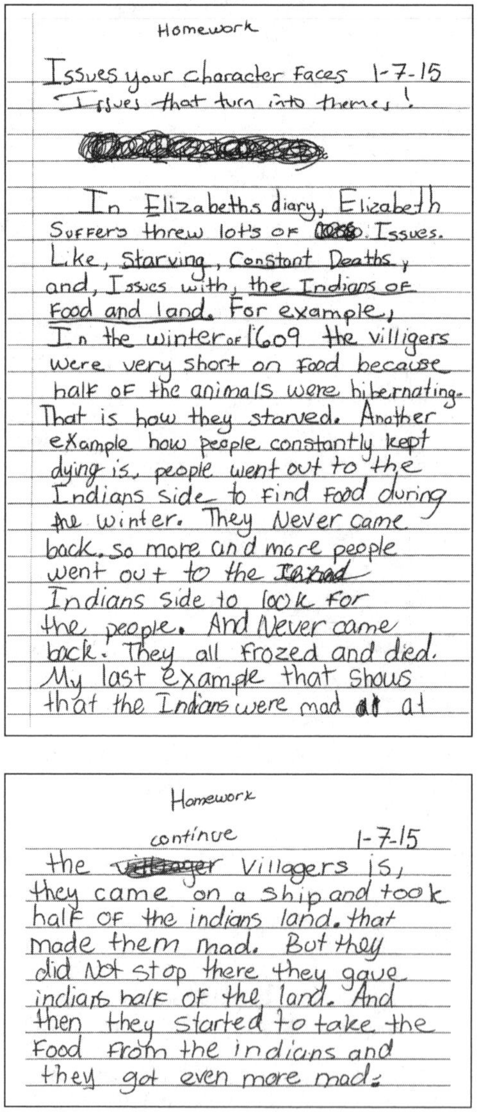

> Homework
>
> Issues your character faces 1-7-15
> ~~Issues that turn into themes!~~
> ~~[scribbled out]~~
>
> In Elizabeths diary, Elizabeth suffers threw lots of ~~[crossed out]~~ Issues. Like, starving, constant Deaths, and, Issues with, the Indians or Food and land. For example, In the winter of 1609 the villigers were very short on food because half of the animals were hibernating. That is how they starved. Another example how people constantly kept dying is, people went out to the Indians side to find food during the winter. They never came back, so more and more people went out to the ~~[crossed out]~~ Indians side to look for the people. And never came back. They all frozed and died. My last example that shows that the Indians were mad at at

> Homework
>
> continue 1-7-15
> the ~~[crossed out]~~ Villagers is, they came on a ship and took half of the indians land. that made them mad. But they did not stop there they gave indians half of the land. And then they started to take the food from the indians and they got even more mad.

FIG. 8–1

Attending to Minor Characters

TODAY, you'll continue the important work of teaching your kids to read interpretively. Tomorrow's session ends the bend and the focus on interpretation, so you have just a little more time to teach into this important work.

This session is designed to help students continue to become more adept at determining themes—at interpretation—by also analyzing perspective. Today, then, deals with two strands of the Narrative Reading Learning Progression. You will help students know the importance of taking more and more of the text into account. Readers continue to ask, "What is this text really about?" and to generate tentative answers, and then they read on, letting those answers evolve and become more complex. So the idea "Annemarie is brave" has already morphed into "Annemarie is forced to be unusually brave," and the idea "War is hard" has morphed into "War makes kids grow up fast."

So today, you will suggest that another way for interpretations to become broader and deeper is to pay attention to the perspectives of minor characters who might otherwise be lost in the shuffle. This message itself—to listen carefully to voices that may be overlooked, perhaps even to the voices of characters that are not likeable—is a valuable one. It is a valuable strategy for understanding more complex texts, and it is also an important step in becoming more critical readers. As students read increasingly complex texts, the story's minor characters and subplots will become increasingly important to understanding the story as a whole, and understanding how and why events unfold. Often, especially in historical fiction, characters other than the main character play important roles. It is Peter, Uncle Henrik, and Annemarie's mother, for example, who play significant roles in getting the Jews, including the Rosens, safely out of Denmark. Annemarie is caught up in the actions of these minor characters. To add to the complexity, Annemarie also plays a role in a subplot of a bigger historical plot (Lois Lowry is such a good writer!).

Today, you will show kids that a reader can read a story in a way that brings out the unspoken thoughts of minor characters. Just because the author does not spell out what every person is thinking doesn't mean that there aren't sufficient clues for the alert reader to read between the lines. This means that one of your first goals is to help students

IN THIS SESSION, you'll teach your students that one way readers broaden or deepen their interpretation of a text is to take into account the perspectives of minor characters.

GETTING READY

- ✔ Prior to this session, read aloud Chapter 9 of *Number the Stars*. You will revisit this chapter in today's session. You will have to pick up the pace so that you will be done reading aloud *Number the Stars* by Session 15.

- ✔ You may wish to practice for the read-aloud/think-aloud you do in the minilessons (see Teaching and Active Engagement).

- ✔ Update the anchor chart "Readers of Historical Fiction . . ." (see Link).

- ✔ Distribute the "Analyzing Perspective" strand of the learning progression to students (see Link).

- ✔ You may want to collect conversational prompts to provide to students (see Conferring and Small-Group Work).

notice the perspective through which a story is told. Then, you will want to help them realize that one way to experience a story deeply and to grow important ideas is to deliberately consider the perspective of a character whose voice is relatively absent in the story. In *Number the Stars*, for instance, we are shown the night when the soldiers come to arrest the Rosens from Annemarie's perspective. We naturally sympathize with Annemarie, Ellen, and their families, and it is not hard to imagine their perspectives. We can imagine Annemarie's mother's perspective—the grief she must have for her own lost daughter, Lise; her fierce wish to protect Ellen, the daughter of family friends; and the hope that her own family will be preserved. It's more of a stretch, though, to imagine the perspectives of the German soldiers, because we have been given no access to their inner emotions, beyond a smile at a child or a chuckle. That smile and that chuckle are significant, though, because they hint at a complex humanity woven into the menacing behavior shown in different scenes.

This is one of those times when Reader's Theater, even in a small way, can bring alive the voices and perspectives of characters and help students to step into their shoes. In fact, you'll see in the lesson that your students (and you) will do some improvisation to act out characters' roles. In the end, this work matters tremendously—and not simply for the insight that your readers will gain into the stories they are reading. Our understanding of ourselves and of others is constrained by the perspectives that are available to us. When we read, our natural sense of empathy is developed as we imagine unfamiliar perspectives, again and again and again. It is important to teach students to read with this intent, and also to carry perspectives they gain from books into their own lives as they strive to see the world differently and to cultivate a sympathetic imagination.

Attending to Minor Characters

CONNECTION

Tell students a story of being introduced to something by two different people, outlining how this gave you two different perspectives.

"Readers, the first time I walked into this school building, guess who was my guide? A first-grader! I happened to run into my neighbor's little daughter by the front entrance. 'I'll show you around,' Susie said, leading me first to the older kids' lockers, and then the playground. 'My friends and I play under *this* tree,' she said. 'The younger kids play in this end of the yard.' Then, pointing self-importantly to one swing, she added, 'This is the swing I fell from last week, and I got a bloody knee.' Almost as an afterthought, she gestured toward the teachers' lounge and added, 'In *there*, though, is where *you'll* probably go at recess.'

When I spoke of Susie's tour, my voice reflected a first-grader's carefree tone. I will change my voice to alter the mood into more officious seriousness when I begin my account of seeing the same school through the principal's eyes. In this simple way, I cue kids to the contrast between the two perspectives. Of course, you should feel free to alter this story to reflect any experience you've had where two perspectives are clearly defined.

"Then, readers, I met the principal who gave me the official tour of the school. Pointing to her office, she said, 'Here's where you'll find me, and here are the mailboxes and bulletins about whatever new programs are coming our way. We also post reminders beside the mailboxes.' Her tour started with an area that Susie had bypassed altogether. The tour included a visit to the reading specialists' office, the book room, and to the inside of the teachers' lounge. She handed me class lists, introduced me to staff, showed me *her* side of the school.

"Readers, it was fascinating to see the same school in two totally different ways. Susie and the principal had such different perspectives from which they viewed the school. I bet that if a tiny worm had shown me around this school, I would have been given access to a different perspective altogether." In my best little-worm-imitation voice, I droned, "To avoid getting trampled under kids' feet, you can hide under this staircase. Under this cafeteria ledge, you'll find the best crumbs."

Teachers, at this point, my story feels fairly sufficient in having done the work of a standard connection. I can slide into a teaching point from here, but choose not to. Instead, I want to invite students into a quick role-playing, helping them to imagine firsthand what it is like to alter perspectives.

Ask students to consider how they'd approach a task. Then have them consider how someone unfamiliar and dramatically different from themselves might perform the same task.

"Imagine that you have to give someone a tour of this school. Think about a quick plan. Where will you take them first? What parts of the school seem most important to show them?" After a minute, I intervened, "Now, readers, think about or jot another tour. This time, imagine how you'd give someone a tour of this same school if you were a bird and your nest was in one of the school trees. What points of the school would you introduce a newbie bird to?" After a few seconds, I prompted softly, "Remember, you're a bird now. Your view is aerial, or from above. You wouldn't notice a

Of course, it's an option to channel students to write rather than to simply think. If you elect this option, you probably won't ask them to also role-play.

hiding spot under the stairs like the worm. Instead, you'd be looking down at stuff. What would stand out to you?"

After a minute, I said, "Partner 1, act out to Partner 2 what you might be saying as *you* start taking a new kid on a tour of the school. Are you ready? Go!"

After just a minute, I intervened and said of the hubbub, "Now Partner 2, act out what a bird might be saying as she gives another bird a tour of this school. Go!"

Review the notion that while it is natural to view the world through a familiar perspective, the deliberate adoption of unfamiliar perspectives will often allow insight into themes that students may have missed the first time.

"Partners, I got the feeling that it was easier to role-play giving a tour as yourselves than it was to role-play giving a tour as a bird, right? Of course, it's easy being ourselves, because we *know* our own thoughts and emotions. We know our perspective. Imagining a bird's thoughts isn't as easy, right?"

"Over the past few days, readers, you've been thinking about what your books might really, *really* be about. Today, I want to show you how stepping into the shoes of a minor character, imagining a perspective you have not considered before, can help you expand your interpretations."

❖ **Name the teaching point.**

"Today I want to teach you that minor characters are in a story for a reason. They, like the main character, help to carry the big messages or big ideas of the story. One way to improve your interpretation of a story is to reread, trying to understand the point of view—the perspective—of a minor character, then to revise your interpretation to include what you learn."

TEACHING

Review the notion that while it is natural to view the world through a familiar perspective, the deliberate adoption of unfamiliar perspectives will often allow new insights.

"Fourth-graders, you saw how easy it was to think about how you might give someone a tour of the school and how it was much harder to imagine how a bird might do this. In the same way, it is usually easy to understand the story from the perspective of a main character and much harder to step into the shoes of another character. Today though, I'm suggesting you give this a try."

Maxwell

• Over here is the play ground do not land there they will try to grab you.

• On the roof you will find the most privecy from the not flying (either) les birds

• Out near the picnic tables outside is were you get your lunch.

• Do not go in to the invible wall or you will smash into it

• Stay Stay Away From The Humans!!

FIG. 9–1 Maxwell takes on the voice and perspective of a bird, giving a bird's-eye tour and some advice.

The notion of perspective is fairly abstract. Children often don't really understand it until they've tried to imagine the world, or one scene, through someone else's point of view. If you find the line between point of view and perspective is blurred, know that you aren't alone. Point of view refers to whether a text is written in a first person's point of view, or a third person's point of view. Who is telling the story? Whose inner thoughts does the reader have access to? Perspective relates to the reasons that a particular person thinks and feels and judges as he or she does. It is important for kids to learn that a person's perspective comes from his or her place in the world, as well as from other things.

Model thinking about perspective in your class read-aloud. Ask students to think along with you as you consider perspectives other than the main character. Then demonstrate bringing Uncle Henrik's perspective alive.

"Let me show you what I mean. In *Number the Stars*, Lois Lowry tells the story through the point of view of one character. When reading any book, you can figure out whose perspective is represented by asking questions like 'From whose eyes do I see all the other characters?' and 'Whose thoughts do I especially hear and know about?'

"Think for a second. Whose voice do we hear in *Number the Stars?*" After a pause, I said, "If you're thinking Annemarie, you're right. The book is written from Annemarie's perspective. But there are other characters, and the skilled reader can imagine other perspectives.

"I'm going to read an exchange between Annemarie and her Uncle Henrik. Annemarie has just realized that the 'sad event' of Aunt Birte's funeral is a lie, so she goes to her Uncle Henrik in the barn where he's milking the cow. All we know about this uncle is that he is unmarried and he's a fisherman—but let's do what we did when we thought about the bird's perspective—let's try to think of his point of view. As I read, let's actually step into Uncle Henrik's shoes, to imagine we are him, in this moment."

> [Annemarie] wandered to the barn where Uncle Henrik was milking Blossom. He was kneeling on the straw-covered floor beside the cow, his shoulder pressed against her heavy side . . . Annemarie leaned against the ancient splintery wood of the barn wall and listened to the sharp rattling sound of the streams of milk as they hit the sides of the bucket. Uncle Henrik glanced over at her and smiled without pausing in the rhythm of milking. He didn't say anything.

Looking up from the read-aloud, I started thinking aloud, as Henrik. "I'm busy with the cow, but really, I've got a lot on my mind. A lot is happening that I have to think about. I make a point of smiling at Annemarie, though. Maybe I am trying to hide my worries, to protect her from what's worrying me."

> Through the barn windows, the pinkish light of sunset fell in irregular shapes upon the stacked hay. Flecks of dust and straw floated there, in the light.
>
> "Uncle Henrik," Annemarie said suddenly, her voice cold, "you are lying to me. You and Mama both."
>
> His strong hands continued, deftly pressing like a pulse against the cow. The steady streams of milk still came. He looked at her again, his deep blue eyes kind and questioning. "You are angry," he said.

Looking up again, I thought out loud on Henrik's behalf. "I seem to be staying pretty calm. Maybe I'm thinking, 'I guess I've been *expecting* this. My niece is smart. What am I going to say about the whole Aunt Birte thing?'"

> "Yes. Mama has never lied to me before. Never. But I know there is no Great-aunt Birte. Never once, in all the stories I've heard, in all the old pictures I've seen, has there been a Great-aunt Birte."
>
> Uncle Henrik sighed.

Because you will have just spent some time engaged in an activity that was not obviously connected to reading, it's important to funnel kids' attention back toward reading now. It will put the school tour perspective activity clearly into a reading perspective, and it will help your teaching point resonate. This also is a place to try to link today's teaching with the flow of the unit up until now.

Throughout this read-aloud/think-aloud, as you fill in the missing inner thinking for Henrik, you'll aim to show children how this work helps you see another dimension to the story, how it adds to the thematic work you've already done.

As you read this text, show the way in which you draw on the text to imagine the perspective of minor characters.

> Figuring Out
> PERSPECTIVE 👓
>
> • Whose eyes are seeing this story?
>
> • Whose thoughts am I hearing?
>
> • Whose voice is telling the story?

Looking up, I thought aloud, again as Uncle Henrik, "She knows something is up. She wants an explanation. Let me think. How do I deal with this? She's just a kid. I don't want her to have to know all this stuff. It puts her at risk. She's a kid." Then, still as Uncle Henrik, I said, "My mind is made up."

> At last he turned to Annemarie as he wiped his own hands with the cloth.
>
> "How brave are you, little Annemarie?" he asked suddenly.

ACTIVE ENGAGEMENT

Continue reading, but now set kids up to take your place, articulating what the minor character is probably thinking and feeling. Give children just tiny intervals for this work.

"Let's give you a chance to try this. I'll read, and you prepare to express Uncle Henrik's thoughts."

> She was startled. And dismayed. It was a question she did not want to be asked. When she asked it of herself, she didn't like her own answer.
>
> "Not very," she confessed, looking at the floor of the barn.

I asked students, "What is Uncle Henrik thinking? Pretend you are him and say his thoughts aloud." A minute later I added, "Draw on everything you know about Uncle Henrik in order to imagine his thoughts, his perspective. Remember his age, his job, his relationship to Annemarie. Use all that to help you slip into his shoes, his perspective."

Children voiced their thinking to each other, many of them talking about how Uncle Henrik might be preparing for how he'll explain things to Annemarie, or how he still might not be sure if he'll lie or tell her the whole truth.

I continued reading:

> Tall Uncle Henrik knelt before her so that his face was level with hers. . . .
>
> "I think that is not true," Uncle Henrik said. "I think you are like your mama, and like your papa, and like me. Frightened, but determined, and if the time came to be brave, I am quite sure you would be very, very brave."

"Turn and talk! What might he be thinking?"

I listened as kids said things like "She can handle the truth" and "I can't protect her. She's gonna have to grow up fast." I continued reading.

> "But," he added, "it is much easier to be brave if you do not know everything. And so your mama does not know everything. Neither do I. We only know what we need to know.

Notice that you'll want to draw on your sense of what this story is really about to bring out the perspective that is implicit but not explicit in this scene.

The "Analyzing Perspective" strand of the learning progression suggests that fourth-graders not only need to do the work of imagining a character's perspective, but that it's also important for them to use everything they know about a character's age, role, relationships, etc., to do this.

Teachers, a think-aloud of this nature in which a character comes to life is guaranteed to be attention-riveting for children, but do remember that you'll want to lodge all this firmly into the larger work of this bend—that of developing children's interpretive skills. The upcoming portion of your lesson, therefore, will need extra emphasis. Remind yourself that getting into Henrik's head and considering his perspective was not merely a fun and interesting activity. It was a specific strategy that can be used to interpret the story more deeply.

"Do you understand what I am saying?" he asked, looking into her eyes.

"Think what he is thinking," I said. "What do you know about Uncle Henrik? Use that to help you *be* him." After giving the children a moment of silence, I nodded, as if agreeing with them, and voiced what I assumed his thoughts must be: "I've changed her life by telling her, but I had no choice. It's this war that's taken my choices away."

Now shift back to interpretation and idea development, pointing out to kids how their new understanding of minor characters can broaden and deepen their interpretations.

"Readers, the last time we talked about the themes that are emerging in this text, many of you said that you thought that the war was making Annemarie grow up fast—she had to be very brave. The point of today's minilesson is that if you take the minor characters into account, your thinking expands. Turn and talk once more. How does your interpretation change based on the information you got from stepping into Uncle Henrik's shoes?"

I listened in as students spoke, then called them back together to share out the general consensus: that Uncle Henrik's perspective provides more evidence to support the idea that war makes Annemarie grow up fast and forces her to be brave.

LINK

Send children off to read, inviting them to attend to the minor characters in their books, as part of their thinking work.

"Readers, today you did two important kinds of work. You learned that you can expand your thinking by attending to—really empathizing with—the experiences and perspectives of minor characters. You also learned something about analyzing perspective as you read—and that relates to a strand on the learning progression. I'm going to distribute copies of that strand for you to keep out on your desk as you work.

"At the end of reading time, today, you'll be able to pause and see what new thinking you've come to, and to think about whether attending to your minor characters and thinking about why they see the world as they do, has given you new insights about the book as the whole."

ANCHOR CHART

Readers of Historical Fiction . . .

- Read analytically, studying parts that clue them in to the facts, feelings, or setting
- Collect and organize key facts: *who, what, where, when, why, how*
- Keep track of the major character's timeline, the historical timeline, and how they intersect
- Realize that a character's perspective is shaped by the times and his/her roles
- Determine themes and support them with evidence from across the story
- Lodge big ideas in small moments, small details, and objects
- **Take into account the minor characters**

Take into account the minor characters

Seeing Whole Texts, Rather Than Small Sections, in a Fresh Light

TODAY'S WORK on considering the perspective of minor characters is work that can invite readers to reread, with new eyes, and it can help children read forward with new complexity.

Whichever lens a reader brings to a text, you'll want to encourage that reader to articulate how an idea runs across their whole novel rather than a section of the book. That is, kids will often describe an idea by only talking about the part of the book they just read. You can show them how to write that idea on a Post-it, and go back to the beginning of the book, using that Post-it as a new lens to reconsider earlier parts. Often, students will see new significance in earlier parts. When I did this work with the Allies club, for instance, they had just recently come up with a new idea, which was "When life is ruined by war, people find ways to survive." First, I complimented these readers on how they were looking not just at the single main character but at "people." The children, though, were only talking about how their most recent chapter supported this idea, which was natural, as they had just come to this thinking. When pushed, though, to take that idea as a lens back to the beginning of the book, they quickly scrawled more responses, and were soon bursting to share these.

MID-WORKSHOP TEACHING   **Readers Add to and Revise Their Thinking, Using Post-its to Help Track New Thoughts**

"Readers, eyes on me for a moment." I was holding a piece of paper on which I'd affixed a large pink Post-it with several Post-its spread out beneath it; lines connected each smaller Post-it back to the large pink one. "I call this a *theory web*," I said. "Do you see the way I've written our idea, our theme, across the pink Post-it and then collected lots of smaller Post-its all around it?" I put the pink Post-it under the document camera to show the students that I had written "War forces you to grow up fast."

"Underneath this big theme, we've been collecting evidence to support this theme of ours. For instance," and I pulled one Post-it from the sheet of paper, "this one that tells about the time Annemarie had to act brave when the soldiers stopped her, Ellen, and Kirsti on the street." I put the Post-it back where it belonged and pulled another from the sheet. I put it on the overhead so all the students could see it. "Uncle Henrik wishes he didn't have to tell Annemarie about Aunt Birte and make her scared but he believes in her bravery."

"I wrote this Post-it after our lesson today because we had decided that after stepping into Uncle Henrik's shoes, we were able to further support our theme about war forcing people to grow up fast. But here's the thing. This Post-it also makes me want to *add* to our theme. When we stepped into Uncle Henrik's shoes, I realized that war also makes people do things they don't want to do—things they are scared to do or wish they didn't have to do."

I picked up a marker and my pink Post-it and modeled adding to my interpretation. "So maybe our new interpretation could include this. Maybe it could say something like: 'War forces people to do things they don't want to do (like be brave, lie to people they love, or grow up fast).' Do you see how I did that? How I used the information I got from stepping into Uncle Henrik's shoes to revise our interpretation?"

I asked students to take out their own books and theme Post-its and try the same work—either adding new evidence to support their theme or revising their theme based on their newest thinking.

You may want to consider giving children a tool to lay alongside them as they have these conversations—a collection of conversational prompts that can get them started on their thinking.

These kinds of sentence starters can go great lengths toward raising the level of students' thinking, as they send students down a particular path armed with the language to develop and express ideas, all the while demanding that kids investigate their ideas by going back to the book.

Revising Interpretations to Include More of the Book!	Gathering Evidence to Include More of the Book!
Readers say...	Readers ask...

Readers say...

- Things have changed a bit from the beginning.... Early in the story, readers see....

- It seems as if there's a pattern.... Earlier readers saw.... This _____ has returned often in their book, for example....

- At first it seemed as if..., but now it seems more like....

Readers ask...

- where, specifically are you seeing that?

- what in the story makes you say that?

- let's look at those parts together...

- let's really compare these pages...

- what in the book, specifically, lets us see this change?

Raising the Level (Right Now!) of Our Thinking about Perspective

Set your readers a task.

"Readers, will you try something for a moment? Will you, and a partner, right now think of a moment or an object on which two characters in your novel have different perspectives? Like Annemarie and Mrs. Rosen had different perspective on the German soldiers at the start of *Number the Stars*. Annemarie finds them annoying; Mrs. Rosen finds them terrifying. In the picture book *Corduroy*, the little girl and the mother have different perspectives about the bear that is missing a button. Give me a thumbs up when you have two characters, and something around which they have different perspectives. If you need an idea from a club member, whisper in."

I waited a moment. "Quickly, jot the two names, and whatever it is on which they have different perspectives." I gave them a second to do this. "Now will you and your partner discuss what influences these perspectives? Why do they think so differently about this item, or this moment?"

I listened for a moment and then interrupted. "Eyes on me. I'm going to give you some tips about how you can raise the level of your thinking about perspective—and all of this relates to that strand of the learning progression." I showed students a list of ways readers can think well about a character's perspective:

To understand a character's perspective, I thought about how . . .

A character's role in life might influence what he or she sees, feels.

A character's past might influence what she or he thinks, feels.

A character's group membership might influence what he or she thinks, feels.

A character's place—the setting—might influence what she or he feels, thinks.

"Go ahead, right now, choose one item on this checklist, and add to your discussion."

They did.

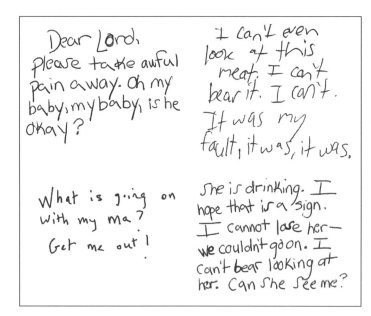

FIG. 9–2   A whiteboard containing the ideas from four readers

I listened as the group came to the decision that one big thing that was happening in this passage is that everyone is frightened about what will happen to the family. They referred to that claim—that everyone is frightened about what will happen to the family—as their "big text Post-it."

SHOW HOW YOUR BIG IDEAS ABOUT YOUR CLUB BOOK HAVE CHANGED

Readers, tonight, as part of your homework, go back to the big tent idea your club had about your book a few days ago. Make a chart or a piece of writing that shows how your thinking is changing. Maybe you used to have one idea and now have several. Or maybe you used to have a particular big idea and now it has changed.

If you want to expand your big idea even further, think about a minor character. From his or her perspective, what is the book really about? Then add those thoughts to your big tent idea.

One way or another, in addition to reading for forty minutes tonight, think about how all this talking and thinking has taken you on a journey of thought.

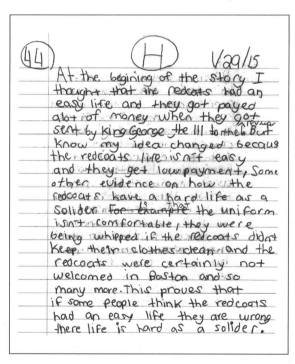

FIG. 9–3   Emma changes her thinking as she learns more about some of the characters in her story.

Self-Assessing Using Qualities of a Strong Interpretation

IN THIS SESSION, you'll teach your students that as readers build interpretations, they draft and revise their ideas by comparing them to qualities of a strong interpretation.

GETTING READY

✔ Prior to this session, read aloud Chapters 10 and 11 of *Number the Stars*.

✔ Show an image of a painting that you love so as to highlight the process of revision. We are using a Seurat painting, *A Sunday Afternoon on La Grande Jatte*. A link to the Art Institute of Chicago website is in the online resources (www.artic.edu) (see Connection).

✔ Before this session, provide students with copies of the poem "Things" by Eloise Greenfield, and ask them to write a quick first interpretation of it. It may be helpful to have scrawled one interpretation onto chart paper (see Teaching and Active Engagement).

✔ Distribute the "A Theme . . ." chart that names qualities of good interpretations (see Teaching and Active Engagement).

✔ Remind students to have on hand the "Determining Themes" strand of the learning progression.

✔ Provide Post-its with the qualities of good interpretations jotted on them (see Link).

✔ Share the "Talking and Writing to Learn" chart (see Share).

✔ Select a few strands from the learning progression such as "Analyzing Perspective," "Inferring about Characters and Other Story Elements," or "Analyzing Author's Craft" (see Homework).

T ODAY you'll again lean on the "Determining Themes/Cohesion" strand of the learning progression to teach students about the qualities of a good fourth-grade interpretation. You will suggest that they use these as guidelines to revise and improve their interpretations.

In addition to guidelines, you will also share models of strong interpretations and set students up to revise their own interpretations. Just as most writers admire the work of published authors and then try to incorporate a few of those craft elements into their stories, readers also profit from having models that help them to revise their initial work.

There are a few things to keep in mind as you prepare this lesson. The first is that in the teaching and active engagement of the lesson, you refer to a poem by Eloise Greenfield. You'll want to read this poem ahead of time so that you can quickly move through it with children. Also, prior to this lesson, ask children to write a quick flash-draft interpretation of the poem.

In the connection of the minilesson, you'll refer to a painting. Your point will be that just as artists studied the Masters, so readers and writers need to study the masters. You'll suggest that learning a craft by apprenticeship has gone on for thousands of years. Cézanne, when he first went to Paris, spent half of each day in the Louvre, practicing what the Old Masters before him had learned to do with ease. Rembrandt taught him to draw. Titian taught him about color. Goya taught him to put his soul into his paintings. And aspiring readers and writers learn from professionals in similar ways.

Reading, too, is something that benefits from mentors and models. People can study what others do as readers and then deliberately set out to work in similar ways. Your kids don't have a Rembrandt of reading interpretation to model, but they do have the Narrative Reading Learning Progression for guidance. This tool will help them self-assess their work and strive to improve it in specific ways. You'll note that in the learning progression, the skills for fourth grade for "Determining Themes" are as follows: I read, asking, "What's this story really about?" and I come up with tentative ideas that I test as I read on. I have an internalized checklist of what makes a good interpretation—that the theme applies to most of the story, and that it suggests a life lesson.

I know that often the theme becomes clearer at the end, but then I can look back and see them trace through other parts, such as times when a character makes a decision or realizes something big. After deciding on a theme that is important to a story, I can find textual details from across the text that support that theme.

"You'll suggest that learning a craft by apprenticeship has gone on for thousands of years."

While this work should be familiar to students, the lesson progresses as a shared inquiry, with you guiding students through the teach and active engagement, offering scaffolds as needed.

Self-Assessing Using Qualities of a Strong Interpretation

CONNECTION

Show your students a work of art, and tell the story of its creation, highlighting the fact that great work is the result of rough drafts and revision. Describe parallels with the writing process.

"Readers, pull in extra close because I want to show you this amazing painting," I said, and then revealed a reproduction of Seurat's famous masterpiece. "It's called *A Sunday Afternoon on La Grande Jatte*, and it shows a group of people relaxing on an island near Paris.

"Do you see how this painting is created out of tiny dots? The artist Seurat studied light and optical illusions. Then he experimented with painting pictures out of little dots rather than brushstrokes, as artists had done before him. Gorgeous, right? To make this painting, Seurat worked for *two years*, drafting and revising.

"The thing is, any kind of meaningful work takes drafting and revising. When you write stories and essays, you take them through many drafts. You know about the qualities of good writing, so you have almost a checklist in mind as you revise. If you are writing a story, you consider whether your characters are compelling. You make sure there's tension in your story and a setting that sets the stage. If you are writing an essay, you develop a claim supported by reasons and evidence. You revise because you want your writing to be all it can be."

❖ **Name the teaching point.**

"Today I want to teach you that readers also take their interpretations around theme through a process of drafting and revision. One way that readers tackle this work is they have in mind an internalized sense of the qualities of strong theme work—and that guides their revision."

◆ COACHING

Teachers, in other places within this series I have encouraged you to list the many ways in which you can gather your students' attention at the start of a minilesson. You now have a new way to do this! Connecting reading to other arts gives readers a new sense of being part of a tradition.

A large body of research shows that students benefit from being given crystal-clear ideas about what it is they should be aiming to do. Many years ago, Sadler showed that when teachers and students have a clear sense of what constitutes quality, this short-circuits the randomness and inefficiency of trial-and-error learning. Feedback, he found, helps students when it decreases the gap between what they are doing and a commonly held image of what constitutes good work. A problem is that "teachers' conceptions of quality are typically held largely in unarticulated form, inside their heads as tacit knowledge" (Sadler 1989, 127).

TEACHING AND ACTIVE ENGAGEMENT

Tell students that readers are guided by internalized qualities of good interpretations. Turn the learning progression into a tiny list of qualities of a good interpretation. Highlight that interpretations connect with the whole text, are grounded in details in the text, and consider the choices the author made.

"As writers, you know some of the qualities of great writing." I pointed toward charts from the writing workshop. "You carry an understanding of effective stories and essays around with you, so that when you go to revise, you draw on your sense of good writing. But I'm not sure you have that same sense of what makes for compelling interpretations. Think, in your mind, of what you'd say are the qualities of a strong interpretation."

I gave students a minute to think and then said, "I'm pretty sure you and I have in mind similar qualities of good interpretation—because this draws on our 'Determining Themes' strand."

Of course, students have already revised their big-tent ideas about texts. They have been revising their interpretations in most or all the clubs. The children's latest iterations of those ideas were the closest the club had to an interpretation that could now be assessed with the checklist in mind.

A Theme . . .

- Is a big idea that relates to the whole arc of the story.
- Is grounded in specific details in the text.
- Considers the choices the author made.

"That means that when experienced readers think, 'What's this story really about?' or 'What is the theme of this story?' these readers aim to be sure their response relates to the whole arc of the story, is tied to specific details in the story (as well as to a big idea), and answers the question, 'Why might the author have made the choices he or she did?'

"You can use this mental checklist to guide revisions of your early interpretations. Let's do some of this work together, now."

Demonstrate the process of drafting and revising responses to reading. Introduce a short text and an interpretation of it that sums up the moral at the end.

"Earlier today, I asked you to reread this familiar poem—you all know it—and to write a quick first-draft interpretation of it. Let's read the poem again—chorally. As we do, ask yourself again, What is this poem is really, really about?

"When you wrote your interpretations, a lot of them went like this," I said, holding up a page of student writing and reading aloud:

A Theme . . .

➢ Is a big idea that relates to the whole arc of the story.

➢ Is grounded in specific details in the text.

➢ Considers the choices the author made.

FIG. 10–1

"Things," by Eloise Greenfield, is a poem about poetry, and it's about how poetry lasts forever.

"Is that what a lot of you would probably say?"

Examine an interpretation against the checklist of qualities, looking especially at whether the interpretation connects with the whole text.

"So, let's take this idea through some revision, using the qualities that are on our 'A Theme . . .' checklist."

I looked again at it, inviting them to do likewise.

"Let's start with 'It is a big idea (or a theme) that relates to the whole arc of the story.' So, let's look at the theme—'Poetry lasts forever'—and ask, 'Does "Poetry lasts forever" pertain to the beginning and to the middle and the end of "Things"?' Give a thumbs up if you think *all* the parts of the poem are about poetry lasting forever and a thumbs down if you think *only some* parts of the poem are about that."

Once readers have assessed that the interpretation does not pertain to the whole text, suggest that the interpretation needs to be revised so it relates to the beginning and middle as well as the end of the text.

I paused to let the children look at the poem with this question as a lens and nodded as I saw thumbs going down. Then I continued, "Looks like most of us agree that the interpretation 'Poetry lasts forever' doesn't pertain to the whole. The beginning and middle of the poem are about sand castles and candy that are gone now. That means that if we say that this poem is about the idea that poetry lasts, the idea doesn't hold true for the first two stanzas.

"Readers, the point of using a checklist is not just to help you see that you *need* to revise. The point is that it can help you know *how to improve* the interpretation. So we know, now, that we need to revise this interpretation so it fits more of the poem. Let's try that now. Start thinking—jot if you want, and give a thumbs up if you have some ideas for new interpretations. I'll do the same.

"Let's compare our ideas for new interpretations. You go ahead and compare with a partner, and then I'll share mine and we can compare." I gave students a moment to compare their ideas, noting how they tried to reach across more of the poem. Then I gathered them again.

"I like how you were trying to include more of the poem! Listen to this revision, which I heard many of you saying, and give it a thumbs up if it fits the beginning, middle, and end of the poem now, or a thumbs down if it still is only about one part."

Things
Went to the corner
Walked in the store
Bought me some candy
Ain't got it no more
Ain't got it no more

Went to the beach
Played on the shore
Built me a sandhouse
Ain't got it no more
Ain't got it no more

Went to the kitchen
Lay down on the floor
Made me a poem
Still got it
Still got it

Eloise Greenfield

When you ask, "Is that what a lot of you would probably say?" you're frankly looking for students to concur, and you convey this by the way you talk and by the way you nod your head as if to suggest that you're just checking that your assumption is correct. You're going to suggest that a checklist of qualities of good interpretation can make a world of difference to readers with that sort of an interpretation.

You should feel as if this first criterion of a good interpretation is familiar. Look back over the span of this unit; there have probably been ten times when you have nudged readers to go from noticing a part that matters to thinking, How does this connect with the whole text?

I ran my finger down the poem as I spoke. "'Things,' by Eloise Greenfield, is a poem about poetry. It says that in a world where many things—sand houses, candy—don't last, poetry lasts forever." I adjusted the interpretation on the chart paper.

"Readers, we could keep revising this interpretation, using the other items on the checklist. I bet you could come up with some ideas for how to ground this interpretation in more details of the poem, and for a way to say something about choices the author made." I looked around, as if questioning, waiting for nods.

"Let's try just one of those. Let's consider the author's choices. Consider the line that repeats, 'Ain't got it no more.' Eloise Greenfield is a super-famous poet. She knows how to write grammatically correct sentences. So why would she *not* write: 'I do not have that candy anymore'?" I used my snottiest voice as I intoned the grammatically correct line twice. Then I switched to an excited child's voice to repeat the line as Greenfield wrote it. "'Ain't got it no more.' If you have an idea for why Greenfield chose to write the line this way, rather than the 'correct' way, give a thumbs up." I paused, then motioned for them to turn and talk.

"Readers, I hear you saying that Greenfield probably chose to write 'ain't got' instead of 'do not have' because she wanted to capture that child's voice—the perspective of an excited, candy-loving youngster! She does capture that voice of a little kid!"

Name what you have taught in a way that is transferable to another text and another day.

"My real point is that we, as readers, can use tools like this checklist to help us develop an internalized sense of what makes for a powerful reading of a text, *and* we then see ways we can take our first, rough-draft ideas and make those ideas even stronger."

LINK

Point out that in this process of drafting and revision, students' ideas ended up rising to the complexity of the story.

"Readers, as you go off to read today, remember that whenever you are doing important work, whether it's reading, painting, or shooting a foul shot, keeping in mind the qualities you are striving for will help raise the level of your work. You probably have a theme in mind for the book you are reading. Before you get started reading, take a second to record that theme, working to make sure the ideas meet the qualities of a good interpretation theme or as if it were a pair of glasses, and read on, marking passages that support that theme. I know the theme you record may have come from talks you've had with your club—that's fine. But use the "Determining Themes" strand of the learning progression to do your best work with this, and remember to support your ideas with references to the text. I'll come around and help with your work with your book's theme."

You'll find that very often, children find their first draft of a theme at the end of a text. It's not always easy to revise that theme so it pertains to the whole text. Often it helps to remember the start of the text generally captures the problem. A theme that relates to the whole text, then, spans the problem and the solution. Instead of, "Hold onto your family," it would be, "When you feel alone, hold onto your family."

Lead Small Groups to Help Readers Progress on the "Determining Themes/Cohesion" Strand

BECAUSE YOU'VE ASKED READERS to record their thoughts about their novel's theme, you'll be able to skim those quickly and gather groups based on what you see. You may find a few children who are still naming the theme of their book in a single word: hope, friendship. Quickly gather those children and point out that in the third-grade learning progression children make a point of being able to say the theme of a story as an idea, a claim, not just as a word. Give these children sentence starters such as "This story teaches readers that . . ." or "In this story, the author says that when . . . , people should. . . ."

Other children will have settled on a theme that feels like a cliché to you. Perhaps one reader's theme is "You can be anything if you just believe in yourself" and another's is "Make new friends, but keep the old." My general suggestion is to let this go. Don't worry. The important thing will be to see whether the child can talk about the portions of the text that support the theme, and can show how those particular passages do advance that idea.

To help children support a theme, remind them to select passages that best support the theme. They'd benefit from imagining a doubting critic who asks, "How does *that* support the theme?" Readers need to not just produce evidence but to be able to discuss why the evidence they select is particularly supportive of the theme. It helps to use sentence starters such as "It is important to notice that . . ." or "The author could have . . . but instead she or he . . . shows that . . . ."

You may want to show students to look not only to the fourth-grade but also the fifth-grade learning progressions for "Determining Themes/Cohesion" and for "Supporting Thinking with Text Evidence." Help them to understand ways into citing the text with transitions, such as "Early in the novel, readers learn that . . ." or "This is evident when . . . ." Your students will also need phrases that help them to shift from citing the text to discussing it, so be prepared to teach them phrases such as "This illustrates . . . because . . ." and "The words the author used are important. She didn't say . . . , but instead wrote . . . . This shows that . . . ."

MID-WORKSHOP TEACHING
Readers Carry Friends' Voices and Interests

"Readers, I know you need more time to read—it isn't yet time to talk—but I wanted to be sure you read, keeping in mind that readers carry on book conversations in our own minds as we read.

"I know you all have done a lot of writing about the theme that your clubs' novels support. As you read, keeping that idea in mind, remember also that you can also be keeping the voices of your friends in mind. For example, if you are lucky, one of your book club members often listens to your ideas and challenges you, asking, 'What gives you that idea?' and 'But how does that theme connect to (this or that part of the text)?' If you have a club member who presses you like that, you are lucky indeed . . . and you'll want to read with that club member's voice in mind. If you have, on the other hand, a club member who nudges you to say more, who says, 'Can you say more about that?' then get used to carrying that with you as you read. Maybe you have a club member who reminds you to think about the setting, about whether trouble is brewing and what the tone of the setting is, or to notice objects that take on symbolic value. Remember, the whole point of reading with a club is that even when your club is not with you, you hear their voices."

Readers Revise Their Interpretations by Examining Every Word

Ask book clubs to discuss their ideas, allowing those ideas to change and deepen.

"Many of you have been revising your ideas about your books as you read. Now, you may want to discuss in your clubs how those ideas are changing. So meet with your club now. Perhaps you will talk again about this question, 'What is this book really about?' Or it may be that you want to talk about other things that seem important. Keep in mind that your thinking will change as you talk. You may want to use 'I'm learning' phrases like those in the 'Talking and Writing to Learn' chart."

As children talked, I listened in. The American Dreamers club was discussing its original idea from *Letters from Rifka*, "As people move to new places, they hold onto things that remind them of their old home and the people they love." They were now reading *Maggie's Door* and wanted to develop an idea that related to both books. I interjected, "As you reread your idea, think about each word. Ask yourself, 'Are we using the best word here?'" The club then revised their interpretation to refer to *immigrants* who were moving and holding onto objects, not just *people*. Immigrants usually *had* to leave—they had no choice, due to poverty, food shortages, war, or discrimination. Their journeys were difficult and full of struggle, which made the things they carried mean that much more. So the American Dreamers' revised idea became as shown in Figure 10–2.

> **Talking and Writing to Learn**
>
> - I'm changing my mind...
> - I'm starting to think...
> - I'm realizing...
> - So, if that's true, then...
> - Can we try that idea on for a bit? If that's true, then how come...?
> - Could it be that...?

> As immigrants move from their old country to America they hold on to their memories and their love for their old home which helps them because they are struggling so much to have a new life.

FIG. 10–2

USE THE LEARNING PROGRESSIONS TO DO YOUR BEST WORK

Readers, we've focused a lot on interpreting the books you are reading, and thinking about theme. But there are lots of other ways to think about a novel as well. Take a few strands of the learning progression and try doing fourth-grade-level work by writing about your book.

Start with the "Analyzing Perspective" strand. Think first about this question: Whose perspective are you given in your book? Who is telling the story? To understand the perspective you can ask yourself, "Whose inner life do I have access to?" Then think about that person's perspective on some of the big actions in the book, the big events, and ask, "How does what I know about this person's role in life (age, jobs, group membership) help me understand his or her perspective?" Write about that.

Then go to another strand in the learning progression. Perhaps you'll think about "Inferring About Characters and Other Story Elements," or about "Analyzing Author's Craft," and again, do your best fourth-grade-level thinking and writing.

Meanwhile, continue to read up a storm.

Turning to Primary Sources to Better Understand History

IN THIS SESSION, you'll teach your students that historical fiction readers often deepen their sense of an unfamiliar era by studying images—photographs and illustrations from the time period.

GETTING READY

✔ Before the minilesson, read aloud Chapters 12 and 13 in *Number the Stars*.

✔ Have on hand a novel with an unfamiliar setting, such as *Out of the Dust*. Prior to the session, find dramatic images of that setting by photographers such as Dorothea Lange to display to students (see Connection).

✔ Before this session, gather photos of King Christian X on his horse Jubilee and German tanks in Copenhagen. Have small copies tucked into your book to show kids how you keep them close as you read (see Teaching and Active Engagement). 👆

✔ Prepare and display the chart "Synthesizing Nonfiction (Images & Text) into Stories" (see Teaching and Link).

✔ Distribute folders of nonfiction materials to children. We've provided some materials and recommendations on the Online Resources, and of course, you can extend these (see Link). 👆

✔ Display and update the anchor chart "Readers of Historical Fiction . . ." (see Link).

✔ Be prepared to shift students after ten minutes from studying these images with their club members to reading their novels, with these images in mind (see Mid-Workshop Teaching Point).

✔ Distribute copies of "A Theme . . ." chart (see Conferring and Small-Group Work). 👆

✔ Note chart "Use Search Terms to Find Historical Images" is in Digital Resources. You may want to reference it (see Conferring and Small-Group Work). 👆

✔ Prepare "Using Images to Deepen Understanding of What You Read" chart (see Homework).

TODAY you launch students into the final bend of the unit. In this bend, students will turn to nonfiction texts and images, including primary sources from the time period, to deepen their contextual understanding of the historical era of their novels. They do this in large part to understand their characters' historical perspectives. Adult readers do this all the time. When we're reading a novel that refers to Eva Braun, we research to see what she really looked like. If the characters in our novel head out with the Donner Party, we read up on the dark adventures of that unhappy band.

It will help to think about the work adults do, translating that into strategies that students can learn. Reading *Memoirs of a Geisha*, I wanted to see what a geisha looks like. The text referenced something that was so otherworldly that I needed some information. Other times, a text seems to assume a background that the adult reader doesn't have. Reading *The Book Thief*, I checked maps and dates to understand the movement of groups of people in that book. There are times when I get so fascinated by the fictional characters that I end up wanting to read about true people who resemble the fictional ones. How many readers graduate from learning about fictional characters in *Number the Stars* to learning about real people in *Anne Frank: The Diary of a Young Girl*?

You will need to prepare folders of nonfiction materials to give to your students. Over the next three sessions, they will study images, print and digital texts, and primary sources from the time period. This work starts today with students studying images from the time period.

You'll set kids up to use images from the time period they are reading about as a way to quickly engage with this period. An effective way to help kids get ready to read about unfamiliar subjects is to provide some images that will help them visualize. You are literally helping them picture what people looked like, what they wore, and, if you can find the images, what kind of stuff was happening then. With Google Images, the Library of Congress, and myriad museum archives available, primary source historical images are just a click away.

Your children are apt to overgeneralize from one photo, for example, to assume that most kids in a particular era suffered from hunger. If you're worried about overgeneralizing, then choose your images to create a balanced view—include an image of a carefree child to contrast with the somber one.

"An effective way to help kids get ready to read about unfamiliar subjects is to provide some images that will help them visualize."

As you teach today, be mindful that you are supporting cross-text synthesis. Reference that strand of the Informational Reading Learning Progression. You are also continuing to help children with the "Analyzing Perspective" strand.

Turning to Primary Sources to Better Understand History

CONNECTION

Describe feeling a little lost as you read, and then tell how you found some images to help you picture the scenes in your novel.

"Readers, have you ever been reading along, and suddenly you realize, 'I can't really picture this'? It's like you were reading, and everything was fine. Then you realize that you're not really picturing the characters or the place? Or maybe some detail emerges, and you begin to wonder whether you were picturing things all wrong."

I saw a few nods and continued. "When I first read a story set in the Dust Bowl, I kept wondering what the Dust Bowl really looked like. Was it . . . a bowl? Was it a big round ball of dust?" I held up a copy of *Out of the Dust* and saw more nods.

"Readers, you don't have to wonder what things probably looked like. Usually, you can find out. That's the glory of living in an age when so many photographs and illustrations have been archived—that means collected—digitally. If I want to know what the Dust Bowl looks like, I can go to a museum site on a computer. Or I can just go to Google Images and enter 'Dust Bowl photographs.' And *wow!*" I displayed the page of Dorothea Lange photographs and other powerful images that appear with this quick search. "Look at that! It doesn't look like a *bowl* of dust so much as a *sea* of dust. Now I can see what characters in that time were really coping with.

"You can do this too, readers. When you're reading about a time or place you haven't experienced, you don't have to wonder what people and places looked like."

❖ **Name the teaching point.**

"Today I want to teach you that readers of historical fiction often study images—photographs and illustrations—from the time period, synthesizing them into relevant parts of their novels, to understand the time period better."

Notice that readers are engaged in cross-text synthesis, a skill that is actually on the Informational Reading Learning Progression. Fourth-graders need to be able to collect and merge information from two texts. Here, you suggest they can bring maps, photographs, and relevant expository texts to bear on their reading of fiction.

TEACHING

Explain that you tuck related articles, photos, maps into your novels. Illustrate with your demonstration text, showing a photograph that relates to that text.

"Readers, I know you often put Post-its in your books, and then carry your books around, filled with all those notes. Listen up. Not only do I put Post-its into my books, I put other stuff there as well. I might tuck a newspaper article or a photograph or a map behind the front cover of a novel—anything that helps me 'get' my book more. I'll show you a new picture that I recently stuffed into my copy of *Number the Stars*."

The picture I show is of King Christian X of Denmark, riding his horse Jubilee through the streets of Copenhagen. It was taken in 1940. 👏

"I bet you know who this is. It's King Christian X of Denmark and his horse Jubilee. When we were reading about the king riding Jubilee through Copenhagen, I thought, 'Really? Riding a horse through the city?' There's no way I could picture one of our presidents riding a horse through a city, especially a city occupied by the enemy!"

Take students through some of the steps of studying and talking about an image, layering in some technical vocabulary so they'll have language to describe what they see.

"I'm going to show you how readers use images to understand a story more deeply. Right now, we are talking about the way a photograph can enrich reading, and you'll see how the photograph helps with envisioning. But keep in mind that other materials like a timeline or a map or a video could help, too. As I use this photograph to help my reading, will you do similar thinking alongside me? Then you can compare the ways that you and I think between this photograph and *Number the Stars*. After a bit, I'll stop and it will be your turn to go on with this work."

I added, "I'm thinking, 'What part of the novel does this go with?'—aren't you? It reminds me of the part of the book where Annemarie is telling Kirsti about the king. I remember wondering what the king really looked like." I opened the book to that passage and read:

> *King Christian was a real human being, a man with a serious, kind face. . . . Each morning, he had come from the palace on his horse, Jubilee, and ridden alone through the streets of Copenhagen, greeting his people.*

I screwed my face up, as if thinking hard. "When I first read this, I pictured a big, strong horse with big feathers in his mane—sort of a fairy-tale horse. I tried to picture the king. I thought he would wear a crown and a cape like a superhero."

Note that you tell kids that when you first read the text, you pictured things in a way that is dramatically different from the way things are represented in the image. You want to show that your envisioning improves because of the photograph.

I returned to the picture. "The first thing I'm thinking is whether the picture fits with what I had been thinking. So I had been picturing a fairy-tale man and his horse in feathers and capes, galloping through a dark street, like Prince Valiant. But the first thing I notice in the photo is how real it looks and how serious. In the foreground, in the front, there is this tall, serious man riding a big horse. And no, the horse doesn't have feathers, but he is a big, strong horse. He looks proud.

"Next, I try to look at the details, in case they can help me understand the facts of the time. Behind the man on the horse, in the background, I see other people, who look like ordinary people! There's even a girl, here in the right side, trying to pedal a bicycle alongside Jubilee. It's almost like a parade!

"I also try to understand people's experiences, their perspectives. So what am I learning? Danish people ride bikes. Also, they don't have guards separating the king from the people. I can see why Annemarie admires King Christian so much, can't you? No wonder the Danish people loved him! He looks admirable. With all his people following along behind him—that's what I'll picture now when I picture King Christian and Jubilee!"

Debrief in a way that names the strategies you used so that students can follow these same steps.

"Did you see how I first thought about what the picture reminded me of in the book? I even went back to the actual page, to remind myself what I had read, and how this picture could fit into the story. Then I compared what I had been picturing before looking at this image to what I actually see in the image. I took my time, and looked in detail at things in all the parts of the picture. Finally, I thought about how this picture changed my perception of things. In this case, it made me admire King Christian more, and understand why Annemarie and her people loved him so much.

"Do you think you can do this? Would it help you to see some images from the time period?" Lots of nods.

"I jotted the strategies we just used with this picture," I said, pointing at this chart.

Synthesizing Nonfiction (Images & Text) into Stories

- Ask: What part of the novel do outside sources fit with?
- Ask: What part of the novel raises questions?
- Study it: Study the big parts and the details.
- Ask: Does this fit with what I know? Or add to it?

ACTIVE ENGAGEMENT

Set children up to try the work you just demonstrated, practicing looking closely at an image from the time period, using it to deepen their envisioning. Then channel them to compare.

"Let's give you a chance to try this with another image related to *Number the Stars*. There are probably millions of images you can think of that might help us picture Copenhagen during the war. I printed this one of Copenhagen, once the Germans came. It shows tanks rolling into this gentle city." I displayed the picture. ✷

You don't pause to actually call on children during this demonstration, but inviting them to compare their responses engages them in the work. Notice how you layer in some technical terms such as foreground, background, margin. *Also, appreciate how this envisioning leads to new insights about the people in the book.*

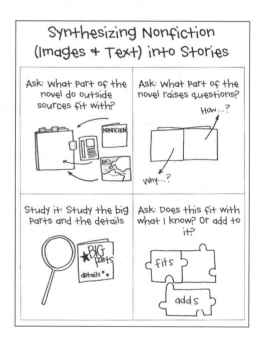

"Why don't you take a moment to study the image, and tell each other what you notice. Remember to ask these questions," and I referenced our chart.

The children, who had been a little open-mouthed as the image sank in, began to talk quietly. As they did so, I voiced over, "Remember to look at all the parts—the foreground and background, the corners and margins."

As children talked, I circulated. After a bit, I voiced over. "I know you aren't holding the book so you can't reread parts it references, but you can think, 'Does this fit with what I know? Add to it?'"

Summarize what children just did, complimenting them on their work and highlighting some insights.

"Readers, I love the way you were so specific and detailed as you described details in the picture. I was especially impressed, though, at how this image moved you. A lot of you said things like 'I hadn't really pictured how awful it was, the tanks, or how scary and dangerous it seems' and 'This picture really helps us imagine how terribly brave Annemarie's family, and Peter, and her sister are. They are fighting against tanks!'"

It's likely that your students are still imagining that the Nazi occupation of Denmark involved a few soldiers on street corners, as they learned about from the opening chapter. This image is shocking. Was this what "a peaceful occupation" of Denmark entailed? This image highlights the courage that Annemarie and her family show, resisting this force.

LINK

Send children off to do this work with their own books and images, specifying that they should spend some time alone with the image(s), before comparing with their club.

"Readers, I know you're eager to do this work with your club and in your own books. In your baskets, you'll find a folder that has a variety of images. I suggest you do these steps. Step 1, gather your club around this folder and lay out the images. There is more than one copy of some of them. Step 2, each of you take an image and think, 'What part of the novel does this go with?' Reread that part. Step 3, spend some time studying the image, using the "Synthesizing Nonfiction (Images & Text) into Stories" chart to guide your work. Work with your club mates to do this."

As students were studying the images from the time period they were reading about, I circulated, murmuring, "Don't forget to read the captions!" and pointing to some of the information that resided there. After a few minutes, I signaled to clubs that they should gather to synthesize their thinking. As they got started, I updated the class anchor chart to include a new bullet:

Readers of Historical Fiction . . .

- Read analytically, studying parts that clue them in to the facts, feelings, or setting
- Collect and organize key facts: *who, what, where, when, why, how*
- Keep track of the major character's timeline, the historical timeline, and how they intersect
- Realize that a character's perspective is shaped by the times and his/her roles
- Determine themes and support them with evidence from across the story
- Lodge big ideas in small moments, small details, and objects
- Take into account the minor characters
- **Turn to nonfiction to deepen understanding**

Turn to nonfiction to deepen understanding

Studying Images to Learn about History

TODAY'S WORK will ignite energy in the room. Students will love the opportunity to see pictures of real-life people and places from the time periods about which they are reading. At the start of reading time, students will huddle around photographs.

You'll probably find that some students need pointers about how to study the pictures in their folders. Just as you've already taught students to linger in parts of a text, you will now want them to linger over parts of the visual images. You might teach them that after an initial look at the whole image, they can take out their pretend magnifying glass and zoom in, one corner at a time, to study the details. You could use the King Christian picture to model how doing this work allows readers to notice—and learn about—so much more than what you first noticed in the minilesson. Now you can notice the cobblestone versus paved streets, the row houses, the everyday dresses and suits men, women, and children wore. Model that you think, "What does this part help me know about the historical time and place?" You will want to use literary language as you discuss the images—terms such as *foreground*, *background*, and *margins*. Then channel students to do similar work with any of the books they have read across the unit.

Children will only be talking together about these images for five or ten minutes, so you'll want to move quickly to reach more than one club. You might remind children that they can read images with lenses they have been applying to their novels. "You can notice the tone, the mood of the setting in a photo, just as you notice this in a novel." Students can also think, "What does the photographer want me to think and feel and know about this time, this place, these people?"

Encourage students to shift between "I see . . ." or "I notice . . ." toward "I'm realizing . . ." or "This makes me think. . . ." With the "A Theme . . ." checklist and the "Determining Themes" strand of the learning progression in hand, you can teach students that the same guidelines apply to *any* interpretation—whether it be about a story, a photograph, a piece of nonfiction, or life in general. Remind them to put together *all* the details they notice, making sure their ideas about the picture connect with the entire image.

If you are teaching with access to at least one iPad, smart phone, or laptop, even if they are your own personal device(s), you might make a center that has one of these devices, and a sheet that has some search terms (see digital resources for this list), so that your readers can begin to search for historical images on their own, with just a bit of scaffolding. You might have Google Images open on your device. In the Digital Resources, we have a "Use Search Terms to Find Historical Images" chart that you might distribute to help students search using terms that will pay off for them.

MID-WORKSHOP TEACHING
Synthesizing Images into Stories

After club members worked for about ten minutes, I said, "Club members, wrap up your book club conversations so you can get some time reading. You'll want to make some decisions about these images before you go back to your own book. Will you keep the image in the folder? Will you put them into your books? Several of these sheets have more than one image—do you want to cut one out and tuck it into a certain page of your book, or your reading notebook? Take a moment to figure that out."

I waited as clubs looked at their images, deciding how they would use them. "Okay, as you go off to read, remember that you might keep some of these images by you, so that on your own, you can decide at a certain point in your reading if an image would be helpful, and then study it for a bit.

"Remember, too, that you're continuing to read, thinking about your characters, and their responses to the setting that you're learning more about. All of that—everything—will relate to the theme of the book, too." I gave the children a few minutes to organize themselves, then channeled them to go off to read.

Understanding a Person's Perspective

Remind readers that the knowledge they gain from studying images of an era can help them understand the perspectives in their books.

"Readers, have you found places in your novel where you say, 'I would never have done what the character just did!'?" Children nodded, and I asked them to tell their club mates about one such time.

"Here is the important thing. As you are becoming wiser about a book and about the era in which it is set, you begin to understand that although *you* might not have acted as a character did, that character had reasons for the actions and choices that he or she made. One of your jobs as a reader is to use all you know from both inside and outside of a book to understand why a character feels or thinks as he or she does. I'm going to give you a few minutes to look back on one of your club's books—and you can use any book you have read—to settle on a time when you and the other members of your club didn't easily understand your character. Think of a time when you thought, 'Huh?'"

After children did this work, I said, "Readers, you'll remember that one of the important skills in this unit relates to understanding a character's perspective. Earlier this year you worked hard to understand the perspectives of not just the Colonists but also the Loyalists before the Revolutionary War. Will you, right now, work together to try to understand the perspective of your character? Remember to think about the reasons why a character might think and feel as she or he does."

SESSION 11 HOMEWORK

 ## USING IMAGES TO HELP ENVISION WHAT YOU READ

Readers, tonight for homework, use images to deepen your understanding of your independent reading book.

Do you have access to a computer or another device and an online connection? If yes, use search terms to find images that might fit some passages in your book. If not, look for images in magazines, brochures, or other publications. I've included a chart of search terms that might be helpful.

Choose a few strong images. Keep them handy as you start reading.

After you examine an image and think about it, jot a few notes. What are your thoughts or insights? Remember to use expert vocabulary to describe the imagery, as suggested in the chart. Think about and answer this key question: How does looking at the image affect how you envision your reading?

Then you can continue with your reading.

Use Search Terms to Find Historical Images

Great Depression	WWII	Civil Rights
• The Great Depression • Great Depression out-of-work photos • Great Depression children working	• WWII propaganda posters • WWII home front • Paris/ Copenhagen/ WWII	• Civil Rights movement • Civil Rights protests • Segregation in America • Civil Rights children's crusade
Immigration	**Westward Expansion**	**Civil War**
• Immigration early 20th century • Immigration to America (Irish, German, Italian, Chinese, or other group) • Immigration Ellis Island	• Westward Expansion • Wagon train • Lewis and Clark • Homestead Act • Pioneer children	• Confederate soldiers • Union soldiers • Civil War photos • Mathew Brady photos

Using Images to Deepen Understanding of What You Read

• Ask: what does the picture remind you of in the book? (Look again at the book.)

• Look at all parts of the picture and notice the details.

• Use expert vocabulary to describe what you see: ~Foreground, background
   ~Margins
   ~Top-left corner, bottom-right corner

• Compare what you had been picturing in your mind to what you see in the image.

• Think about how the picture affects your envisioning of what you read.

Turning Reading into a Project
Add Background Information to Deepen Understanding

IN THIS SESSION, you'll teach your students that readers make their reading into a project, particularly by researching on the run as they read.

GETTING READY

✔ Prior to this session, read aloud Chapters 14 and 15 from *Number the Stars*.

✔ Be sure students have their book club books, with sticky notes and pictures tucked inside (see Connection).

✔ Prepare to read aloud an excerpt from an article about the Danish method used during WWII to fool search dogs that Lois Lowry references in Chapter 15 (see Teaching): www.gratefulness.org/giftpeople/duckwitz_danes.htm. A link to this article is available on the online resources.

✔ Add nonfiction texts related to each club's era into the folders they received yesterday. We've provided resources and links to resources on the Online Resources that accompanies this series (see Link).

✔ Display and prepare student copies of a chart titled, "Historical fiction readers deepen their understanding by . . . ," listing the steps you'll follow today during your demonstration (see Teaching and Homework).

✔ Students will meet with clubs today in the minilesson and at the end of reading time (see Active Engagement and Link).

✔ Prepare to jot a list of good sources for historical information (see Share).

TODAY, you'll continue to teach your students that one way to enrich their reading experience is to connect other related texts to their work with a particular book. If you think of it, you are no doubt doing that very work as you read this unit. You read about a minilesson on the power of looking at images as one reads. Meanwhile, you think, "Oh, this reminds me of that workshop I once attended on teaching kids to read the four quadrants of an image," and you essentially slot that information in between the pages of this book. Then you see the photographs we recommend you use and you recall another photograph related to *Number the Stars* that a colleague shared with her kids last year. That photo, too, gets tucked into this book. Piaget calls that work *assimilation* and *accommodation*—which are really fancy words for learning. A book can act like a file drawer in one's mind, and related knowledge—including information you already knew but hadn't yet linked to the topic at hand, plus new knowledge that you learn as you go forward—essentially gets slotted into that file drawer.

So this means that you will teach your students to see invitations to do bits of research as they read, and the information from that research can essentially be slotted in between the pages of the novel. Here's the powerful thing: The information that kids find does indeed enlarge the actual book, as it becomes furry with Post-its and articles, maps, and timelines—and that information can also enlarge a reader's understanding of a book. This, of course, is especially true for kids who will tend to read historical fiction without bringing the same knowledge of history that you and I bring to the book.

If you had taught this lesson a decade ago, it would be vastly more ambitious than it is now. Today, kids are already working between print texts and digital texts. They already see research as something one does to get the best pizza, the cheapest sneakers. Fourth-graders today are able to access information in ways that doctoral students, a generation ago, couldn't dream of doing. In this session, then, you teach kids to read, alert to the invitations in a book to find out more.

This session can't spell out exactly how kids will do the research that you are hoping they do, because each school will have varying access to devices and the Internet. You'll teach kids that accessing background information is no big deal—it can be as easy as using the X-ray application on a Kindle (what an app!) or doing a Google search on a smart phone. The big point, though, is that to do this work, you become the kind of reader who envisions reading texts outside of the text in hand, and in particular, you turn to quick nonfiction reading. To get children started, you'll hand them enticing texts that will provide them with more background knowledge, but you will also want to help them learn to find resources themselves.

"Fourth-graders today are able to access information in ways that doctoral students, a generation ago, couldn't dream of doing."

Then, too, you'll help them to think about the "Growing Ideas" thread of the learning progression: "I can choose to let the story I'm reading spark ideas as I read. Those ideas might be about the world, other people, a topic I read about, or the story itself. If appropriate, I develop my ideas by paying attention to the text. I use my ideas as a lens for rethinking or rereading."

It is helpful for you to see this session as an extension of all the other sessions in this book. In a sense, the entire unit works *against* the tendency for a reader who can read level U books (like *Number the Stars*) to ignore the detail, the figurative language, the symbolism, themes, subplots, and background knowledge that give that book complexity. (If this reader attends to little more than the bare plotline, she reads in such a way that her level U book becomes a level M book.)

So far, students have done a lot of work to see and wrestle with complexity in their novels. They've disentangled multiple plotlines, they've worked to attend to unfamiliar settings, they've discerned underlying ideas that are central to the overall significance of the story, they've investigated multiple perspectives, and they've thought about the role that minor characters play. All of this helps students honor the complexity of their books. Today's session continues that emphasis.

If you haven't yet filled up the folders of nonfiction materials for clubs, be sure you've added enough nonfiction texts for them to do some quick reading and research today. It's helpful to insert multiple copies of texts, so club members can read individually. You may also, if your classroom has some laptop computers or iPads, bookmark some good sites for kids.

Turning Reading into a Project
Add Background Information to Deepen Understanding

CONNECTION

Tell children that the work they did yesterday, of adding historical images into their books, can extend to print as well.

"Readers, I was thinking about the work you did yesterday. Will you do something for me? Will you hold your books up in the air for a moment?" Soon books were waving in the air. I noted that many had Post-its and pictures sticking out from the books. Some Post-its and pictures slid out of the books.

"Yes, I knew I was right!" I motioned for kids to put their books down. "I was thinking of how yesterday, you made your books fatter, with the notes and pictures you put into them. And I was thinking that it's not just that *the books* are getting bigger, *your reading* is getting bigger. Some people would just read these books for 'what happens'—the plot. But *you're* reading for multiple ideas. And then yesterday you added in extra stuff from *outside* the book, like historical images."

❖ **Name the teaching point.**

"Today I want to remind you that readers don't limit themselves to the book in their hands. Readers gather resources on the run that will deepen comprehension. One important way to do this work is to read texts alongside your novel—texts that add background knowledge."

TEACHING

Point out that readers who shift between reading fiction and reading related texts end up knowing more and thinking more.

"My point is that when you're turning your reading into something bigger, it's not just images that will help your thinking get bigger. You can also shift between reading the novel and reading articles, maps, and timelines. Those texts can provide background knowledge that will help you understand more and think more as you read. Once you have a map beside you as you read, you think about geography. You saw that in our last unit, *Reading History*, and it's true when reading fiction, too."

◆ COACHING

It is an extraordinary thing to sit alongside a child who is reading a book that is set in another time and place, and to ask that child to think aloud, revealing to you what he is imagining. Perhaps the child is reading Skylark, *the sequel to* Sarah, Plain and Tall. *The story tells of the prairie drying up in the drought. "What do you see?" you ask, and come to realize the child hadn't even noticed the words* prairie *or* drought *and had no image of the setting. That sort of research highlights the importance of this session.*

Ask students to note the way you go about bringing nonfiction to bear on a story. This time, start with a question and search for relevant outside texts.

"Watch me as I do some of this work. Will you quickly research the steps I follow and see if they're the same steps I followed when bringing images to bear on a story? Pay attention, analyze what I'm doing. In a moment, you can talk with a partner about how this work is different when we're synthesizing nonfiction into a novel." I displayed the chart "Historical fiction readers deepen their understanding by. . . ."

I began to role-play. I picked up the novel. "So first, I question if there is any part where I've read something and I'm confused. So, is there anything in *Number the Stars*, in the part we've been reading recently, where I sort of go, 'What?'?"

I flipped back through the pages slowly. "You know, I am wondering about that part where the soldiers' dogs begin to growl and sniff at the lunch basket Annemarie is carrying, and suddenly they are sniffing at that special handkerchief Annemarie's mother insisted on putting in the basket.

I read aloud a snippet: "'The dogs lunged, sniffed at it eagerly, then subsided, disappointed again.'"

"This part definitely makes me think 'What?' The question I have is 'What's up with that handkerchief? What made these guard dogs growl like that?' So I found a place where I am confused, a place where I wonder about something. I came up with a question." Then I pointed to the "Historical fiction readers deepen their understanding by . . ." chart, asking students if they were thinking whether my work was progressing in the same way. I knew I'd actually begun this process a bit differently, starting not with a source but with a question—which will soon lead to a source.

"Now, I want to try to answer that question. I have to find some nonfiction that will answer my question. I could do some research on the Web, but this is a file of articles related to *Number the Stars*, so let me start here." I rummaged through the folder. "This article is about the fate of children in the camps. It's interesting, but not relevant. This article is about the fishermen who took Jews to Sweden. It's not all about dogs, but it might have something because in *Number the Stars* it's the fishermen who need this handkerchief. Let me skim it."

In your demonstration, dramatize that the whole text may not be about the research question.

I made a small drama out of skimming the article. After a second I raised my voice. "There is something, halfway through the article. Listen to this . . ."

> In the weeks following the Jewish New Year, almost the entire Jewish population of Denmark—nearly seven thousand people—was smuggled across the sea to Sweden. . . . After the Nazis began to use police dogs to sniff out hidden passengers on the fishing boats, Swedish scientists worked swiftly to prevent such detection. They created a powerful powder composed of dried rabbit's blood and cocaine; the blood attracted the dogs, and when they sniffed at it, the cocaine numbed their noses and destroyed, temporarily, their sense of smell. Almost every boat captain used such a permeated handkerchief, and many lives were saved by the device.

Notice that in this session, as in most of your demonstrations, you set up the way children will watch you as you demonstrate. Notice, too, that you demonstrate a step-by-step process that is transferable to other texts, on other days.

Watch the way in which you go from naming the steps you are taking in ways that are transferable to other texts, to doing the work with this text.

I turned to the kids. "Fascinating, right? Now we need to ask, 'Does this fit with, add to, what we already knew?' I understand the story better now. Annemarie's mother was sending a special handkerchief along, to protect the Hansens from the dogs. And it protected Annemarie too! So I'm wondering how this helps me understand Annemarie's perspective better. Hmm, . . . It's interesting, because she has no idea that the handkerchief is so important, right? Again, her parents protect her from knowing too much. So how can we alter our chart so it explains these ways of working too? Talk to your partner."

Debrief in a way that students can follow your steps, and transfer this strategy to their ongoing reading lives.

I listened in. Then I said, "So now we're realizing that whether the outside source is a photo or an article or a map, you handle it similarly. And you can start with the photo, the article, or the era, or you can start with a novel and some questions you are asking. Either way, the main work involves enlarging your understanding." I gestured toward the process chart.

"Readers, you can do this too, by following these steps. You don't even have to read that much, or read it all perfectly—the point is that you pay attention to when you have questions, and sometimes you put the book down, go find out more, and then go back to the book. It's like you give yourself a crash course on a particular topic."

ACTIVE ENGAGEMENT

Invite club members to consider the kind of questions they have, and the background information that might help them comprehend more.

"Readers, this isn't just *Number the Stars* work. Whenever you read harder books, and often when you read historical fiction, you'll find references to stuff you wonder about. When that happens, you can gather your questions, find some sources, and read on the run. So right now, will you flip back through your book or through your notes? Ask yourself: 'What would I like to know more about?' 'What background information might help my reading?'"

As children began flipping through their books and notebooks, I voiced over, "When you come up with something you'd like to know more about, jot it down. Maybe there's more than one thing. It might be an event in history, or a person who seems to be famous but you're not sure who he or she is. It might be an object that existed back then that you can't quite figure out or identify, like a butter churn or a transistor radio. It might be a place or a date."

After a moment, I signaled to children to turn to their clubs, saying, "Go ahead, share with your club. What are some of the questions you have? What background information would be helpful?"

Historical fiction readers deepen their understanding by...

1. Finding places in the story where they have questions.

2. Looking for a source, including part of a bigger article.

3. Reading just that part to gather information.

4. Rethinking what happened in the book with this info in mind.

LINK

Distribute nonfiction texts to each club, and invite them to reference these texts if they have questions as they read.

"Readers, I'm distributing nonfiction texts that will give you some of that background knowledge on the era your club has been studying. And of course, you can add to these folders. You don't have to read just what I have found for you. You can do some research tonight. For today, get ready to read. Go back to your novels—but if you have questions, know that both the nonfiction articles and the images from yesterday can help you."

I motioned to clubs. "Before you go off, take just a minute with your club to make decisions about whether you have questions to pursue now, or whether the most important thing is to read, knowing your reading might end up channeling you to nonfiction or to photographs or to the globes. Do some quick talking."

Club members talked and I circulated. Soon, most of the clubs had dispersed to read.

Supporting Readers as They Grow Ideas

A S YOU CIRCULATE, pulling up alongside individual readers and bringing together small groups with similar needs, you'll sometimes teach into students' nonfiction reading, sometimes into their reading of historical fiction, and sometimes, you'll help students navigate their movement back and forth between the two.

Because you've just distributed a folder of texts, you'll likely find many students huddled over nonfiction at the beginning of workshop. They left the minilesson with questions related to their novels in hand, but chances are good that the files of source material will have led them to leave their novels behind, so you'll want to help them move between the nonfiction and their novels. The connections between the nonfiction texts and the novels may not be immediately obvious, so help them think about both. What might the implications be of this timeline, this photo? You might encourage them to annotate their documents, underlining important facts and jotting notes in the margins, such as how information connects with what they're reading in their historical fiction books, or what the author wants readers to think or feel about the information. You might encourage them to annotate their documents, underlining important facts and jotting notes in the margins. If you don't want students to mark the texts, they could jot on Post-its or in their reading notebooks.

If you see students recording every detail about a nonfiction text without seeming to make sense of the big picture, you might similarly remind them of strategies they've learned for researching and note-taking. Depending on how the text is organized and what they are hoping to learn, you might again teach students to categorize information into boxes and bullets, but you might also show them how to read looking for the cause and effect of an event, or the sequence of events. Doing so would mean structuring their notes accordingly, helping them prioritize and organize information on the page and in their minds.

Of course, you'll aim to provide appropriate nonfiction texts, but you may notice some students struggling to make sense of them. If that happens, you might remind them to read one chunk at a time, pausing to say what they read in their own words. You might

also encourage club members to read as partners, so they can chunk the text and then discuss what they're learning and what feels confusing.

MID-WORKSHOP TEACHING
Synthesizing across Texts—and across Units of Study

"Readers, do you remember that earlier this year, when you studied extreme weather and the Revolutionary War, you learned a lot about how readers synthesize across texts? Right now, remember what you learned about taking a subtopic that you are learning about in one text, and reading across texts on that subtopic. Tell someone near you three things you learned about doing that work. Turn and talk."

As students talked, I circulated among them, listening in. "Readers, eyes back here. I hear you say that it often helps to start with an easier text. Good point. So if your novel tells about entering the U.S. through Ellis Island and you have four books on Ellis Island, which will you read first? And next?" The children called out, and I signaled with a thumbs up. "I also heard you say that as you read, you ask, 'Does this fit with what I already knew, or is this something that adds onto what I knew?' You will be wise to ask those questions now. I didn't hear anyone say this, but the last tip I want to give you is that if the nonfiction text tells something different than what you expected, that will be interesting. Think, 'Whoa! What could be going on? What could explain this?' I think you will find that there is not just *one* history of an event—that there are many histories.

"Get back to your work, synthesizing between texts. And yes, if you want to bring out that strand from the Informational Reading Learning Progression, that'd be smart!"

Drawing on All You Know to Rehearse for a Club Talk

Channel students to spend a minute rehearsing for the day's club conversation time. Remind them to draw on all they know about reading historical fiction.

"Readers, before you put on a concert or perform a play, you rehearse. It can also help to rehearse a book club conversation. For a few minutes, will you think about the most important questions you think your club might talk about today? Reread your Post-its, scan your book, and do some jotting."

I let students jot for a minute, and then said in a quiet voiceover, "Will you look at our anchor chart from earlier in this unit and from our earlier units, too, and decide whether you are remembering that *all this work* is important? Your nonfiction research should deepen your ideas about the challenges characters face, the life lessons they learn, and not take you away from that interpretive work." Again I let children jot and think, and then I channeled them to talk with their clubs.

As I pulled up to listen to Ali and Jerod, I noticed they were jumping from one person's idea to the next's, developing no one person's thinking with any depth. "Readers," I said, "You are hopping from one topic to the next. Will you remember to use our 'Growing Powerful Book Club Conversations' chart to extend what each one of you says? Aim to linger with and develop one idea for at least five or six minutes."

FIND BACKGROUND INFORMATION TO DEEPEN UNDERSTANDING OF HISTORICAL FICTION

For homework tonight, continue to read your club book, but this time, work actively to fill your book with other texts that relate to it. Find maps, timelines, photos, nonfiction texts, or find parts of other historical fiction books that relate to what you are reading, and slot these into the pages where they are relevant. I'm sending home a sheet with tips on how you can learn more about the historical era in which your book is set (see digital resources) and a copy of the chart, "Historical fiction readers deepen their understanding by. . . ."

As you do this, don't simply think, "Does this fit with what I know? Or add to it?" Also ask, "What can I figure out about people's experiences?"

Curious about history in your books? How to find out more . . .

- Type key terms into Google or Wikipedia. Ex: WWII Danish guard dogs.
- Try museum websites (Tenement museum, Holocaust museum, etc.).
- Check out Google Images.
- Go to the library!
- Let friends and family know what you're studying.

Readers Learn History from Historical Narratives

ear Teachers,

You've been teaching your students that they can research history alongside of reading historical fiction, and that as they do so, the secondary and primary source materials will inform their understanding of their historical fiction, making their books furry with inserted material and making their understanding of the historical era far richer. That's important work for lots of reasons. Your students are continuing to develop their abilities to engage in cross-text synthesis (a skill on the Informational Reading Learning Progression but one of many skills that actually pertain across narrative as well as informational texts). More than this, their understanding of history is deepening. Whether their clubs are studying the Great Depression, immigration to the U.S., World War II, Westward Expansion, Colonial America, the Holocaust, or any other era, you'll see that they are beginning to construct an understanding of that era.

Today, we're inviting you to design your own minilesson, and we want to suggest that you use this as an opportunity to build upon a minilesson many of your students were taught in third grade. Back then, they were reading biographies, not historical fiction, and they learned that they could either bring a lens of story to bear on their texts, thinking about the character who had traits and motivations, encountered difficulties, and so forth, or they could bring the lens of reading for information to bear on those same stories. In that third-grade minilesson, children learned that they read *biographies* through the lens of learning information. For example, if they were reading a biography about a famous violinist who grew up during World War II, besides learning about the subject of the biography, they could also expect to learn a little more about World War II, and probably about playing the violin, too. They could even come away from that biography with boxes-and-bullets notes (and thinking) about violins. This was part of a chart that your students saw when they were in third grade.

- Read the text as information
- What topics can you learn about?
- What are the main ideas and supporting points?

Today you'll point out to your children that they needn't turn to *nonfiction* texts alone in order to learn about history—their historical fiction books, too, will teach them about history, if they read those books with the lens of learning information through them.

You may want to launch the lesson with a connection in which you ask children to share some of what they have learned about the eras in which the stories they've been reading are set. You could, if you wish, return to the idea that you are a conductor of a symphony, and when you tip your baton at one child, that student says one interesting thing the child has learned about the historical setting for their novel. If you decide to do that, give children a moment to look through their notes and prepare so that they'll be ready, at the tip of your imaginary baton, to sing out one choice detail or another.

After the room is filled with choice tidbits that half a dozen children will have shared, name your teaching point. "Today I want to teach you that readers of historical fiction not only shift between reading fiction and reading related nonfiction. Readers of historical fiction also shift between reading their historical fiction as one reads a story, and reading it as one reads an informational text. Because here's the thing—you can learn information from historical fiction."

In the teaching section of the minilesson, you will probably want to remind children that they learned something similar during third grade (as mentioned earlier in this letter). You could point out that just as Jack, in the Magic Tree House series, keeps a notebook and records things in it when he learns about history, your kids can take note of what they learn about history as well. You might say, "Sometimes, when I read Magic Tree House, I think about how my notebook would compare to Jack's. You can do this too—be like Jack as you roam the world of your historical fiction novel. Be alert for what you're learning about history. Jot it down, think about it, talk about it!

"When you cite examples of what Jack learned—and what you learn, too—be sure you do so in ways that accentuate how readers learn not only the fact but also the experience of a historical era. They can learn how devastating the droughts of the 1930s were, and the impact of the Dust Bowl on farmers. They can learn about how people, during the Nazi occupation of Europe, fell into roles of collaborators, resistors, and bystanders. They can learn about the separate schools, bathrooms, and water fountains in the U.S. before the passage of civil rights legislation in the 1960s."

Instead of demonstrating by using *Number the Stars*, you will probably feel as if the students could do with a bit of variety. You might tell them about a student from your class who read his or her historical fiction novel, viewing it as a source of information and insight into an era of history. Show boxes-and-bullets notes that your students took about the era in which the novel is set.

For the active engagement section of your minilesson, you might show a snippet of a video of a historical fiction story, asking children to listen, trying to glean something about the life and times of that era. Show them that even just a few minutes of such a video can yield a lot of insights and information about that time.

As the minilesson comes to a close, remind readers that during reading time that day and always, they can draw on all they have been taught, not just on this day's lesson. There aren't a lot more days in the unit, and surely you want students to remember to do the big work of interpreting the stories they read. You want them to grow big tent ideas, and then read and reread, regarding the text through the lenses of those ideas. You want them to continue to read, alert to times when the text is confusing and to realize that sometimes that confusion should send them off to engage in a quick bit of research. You want them also to know that what they take from a book relates, in a big way, to the lenses they wear as they read.

One of the reasons that historical fiction is as rich and as complex as it is, is that these books are written as big and significant stories and also as important statements about history. In order to accentuate the fact that these novels can teach children information about history, you will probably want to tell children about the amount of research that writers of historical fiction engage in.

You could say, "I was reading about Lois Lowry last night to learn what kind of research she did and how reliable her books were. It turns out she did an interview with Scholastic. Listen to what she said about her research for *Number the Stars*:

> I did a lot of research in libraries, about the history of WWII and Denmark's role in it. But the most important thing I did was to go to Denmark and to talk to people who had actually participated in the rescue of the Jews. It was important, too, to walk around Copenhagen and feel what the city is like (and imagine what it had been like then) and to go up the coast, through the farmland and the fishing villages. (http://www.scholastic.com/teachers/article/lois-lowry-interview-transcript)

On her blog, Lois Lowry tells of receiving a letter from a Danish reader who wrote that he couldn't find evidence of the Danish Resistance using cocaine to confuse search dogs (which happens in *Number the Stars*). Lowry writes: "I became fearful that perhaps I had simply heard the story and accepted it as true, thereby doing what so many other people have done in repeating the myth that the king of Denmark wore a yellow star in sympathy with the Jews . . . but I started looking, and whew." Then she offers the obituary of Dr. Ernst Trier Morch, one of the scientists responsible for concocting the mixture to protect hidden Jews from the German dogs.

When authors do that sort of research before writing historical fiction, surely children will want to read those books not only as stories but also as history.

Sincerely,
Lucy and Mary

Some People's Perspective Is Not All People's Perspective

IN THIS SESSION, you'll teach students that as readers come to know people's perspectives, they are careful not to make assumptions or overgeneralize.

GETTING READY

✔ Prior to this session, read aloud Chapter 16 from *Number the Stars*.

✔ Review the "Analyzing Perspective" and "Critical Reading" strands of the Narrative Reading Learning Progression.

✔ Have a sample of student notes that include overgeneralizations (see Teaching). ☜

✔ Display the anchor chart "Readers of Historical Fiction . . ." (see Link).

✔ Display the "A Theme . . ." chart and "Historical Fiction Readers Deepen Their Understanding . . ." charts (see Conferring and Small-Group Work). ☜

T HE THROUGH-LINE OF THIS BEND is that you can learn history alongside of and through your historical fiction reading. A major goal of the work at the start of the bend was to encourage students to read *around* their novels. So often, children know little of the context for what they're reading—not only in ELA or social studies, but in science. Learning to find out more will stand them in good stead in all their studies.

Yesterday, you taught children that they can also learn history inside of their novels—after all, their authors did a lot of research. The beauty of that work is that readers of historical fiction will, in fact, know more than their peers who don't read. The danger will be that students will overgeneralize. Because the Rosens were saved from the Nazis in *Number the Stars*, they may assume that all Danish Jews were saved. Because Mrs. Rosen has a fearful perspective on the Germans and a trusting one toward her Danish neighbors, they may assume that all Danish Jews shared these perspectives.

Today, you teach children to be more nuanced in their claims and assumptions. Your primary focus will be to highlight the danger of overgeneralizing. One person's perspective, you'll teach, is not necessarily everyone's, not even everyone from that time, place, or group.

This is one of those lessons where your teaching will apply to life as well as to reading. Learning to be cautious about assumptions, learning to be alert to generalizations, is part of learning to avoid stereotyping, and to develop nuanced understandings, and to be more self-critical and questioning.

One Person's Perspective Is Not All People's Perspective

CONNECTION

Tell a story that demonstrates overgeneralization, inviting students to analyze the story with you.

"Readers, I was really glad to see you working to learn history from your historical fiction novels. I saw some of you learning about Ellis Island, about the prairie, about Brooklyn during World War II, about schools during Colonial America. That was good work, but it raised a concern that I want to talk to you about today.

"To do that, I want to tell you about a conversation I overheard at recess. It made me uncomfortable. I think I've figured out why, and I'd love to compare my idea with yours. Will you listen to this conversation, and be ready to say what feels kind of wrong—slightly off—in what was said? And be ready to think, also, about how this has anything to do with your wonderful efforts to learn history from historical fiction. You ready?" I waited for nods.

"Here's how it went," and I used to different voices to represent my characters.

"One fourth-grader said to her friend, 'Look out, some fifth-graders are coming over. They're all really mean. I saw one knock a kid down once and not even say sorry. They don't care about being nice.'

"The other fourth-grader said, 'I know. And they *all* litter too. I saw one throw his juice box on the ground. They don't care about the environment at all, those fifth-graders.'"

I paused, and made a puzzled face. "Something doesn't feel right here . . . what do you think? Share your ideas with your partner and let's compare."

After students had buzzed with outrage for a moment, I interrupted them.

"Fourth-graders! I can hear that you are outraged that these kids were making claims about *all* fifth-graders, based on one fifth-grader's actions and perspective. I'm not sure if you know these terms yet, but that's called *making assumptions*, or *overgeneralizing*."

Name the teaching point.

"Today, I want to teach you that as readers research characters' perspectives, it's important to recognize that one person's perspective is not everyone's perspective. Readers, therefore, are cautious about making assumptions and overgeneralizations."

TEACHING

Give students an explicit tip for avoiding overgeneralizations. Then invite them to study some student notes.

"Here's one tip to help avoid overgeneralizations: Be specific! Here's a second tip: When unsure, ask, 'Who are we really talking about?'

"When you study the story of the members of the Danish Resistance during the Holocaust, you are not learning about everyone in the Holocaust. You are learning the points of view, the perspectives, the stories of the people who are represented in the novel you hold. What you learn from *Number the Stars* about the Jews in Denmark will not be true for the Jews here in the States, for instance. What you learn about Bud's perspective during the Great Depression might not match another child's perspective, or an adult's perspective, from that period.

"Let me show you what I mean. I'm going to put on my special 'history glasses.'" I acted out picking up a pair of glasses. "I'm going to share some imaginary notes that two different kids could have written. These are notes like Jack's, only they capture what two different kids learned about history from reading *Number the Stars*. I typed them up for you. Can you study these notes with a partner, and see what you notice? Be ready to give your thoughtful judgment on this work." I handed out the sheets to partners.

Chapter 8–Chapter 10   NOTES BY ELIZA
Using My History Lens

I notice these details . . .	I learn . . .
• p. 68 Annemarie talks about not having cream in the city. They get cream in the country.	• <u>Everyone</u> in the country had a lot of cream and butter. They just ate butter all day. In the City, no one had any cream or butter.
• p. 77 Uncle Henrik explains that it's better if not everybody knows everything and that sometimes they have to lie.	• Everybody lied during the war all the time. It was just lies, lies, lies.

You'll notice that the contrast between one set of notes and the other is exaggerated—that's on purpose, so children can easily see the difference between them. When kids are in fifth grade, if they're in our writing units, they'll learn to use qualifiers in their claims and evidence—to claim, for instance, that most *instead of* all *do or think something. Here, you edge them toward that work, nudging them to notice and remember the specificity of what they're reading.*

Chapter 8–Chapter 10   NOTES BY THOMAS
Using My History Lens

I notice these details . . .	I learn . . .
• p. 68 They get cream and butter from Blossom.	• People in the country who could keep a cow could eat better—like eating cream and butter. In the City, families like Annemarie's who used to have cream and butter now missed having it.
• p. 77 Uncle Henrik explains that it's better if not everybody knows everything and that sometimes they have to lie.	• The war made some families careful and tricky— especially with what they told children.

The children bent over the notes, poring over them. Soon, conversation erupted, as students responded to the exaggerated generalizations.

Gather students' attention and summarize their comments, reiterating the nuanced work of reading to learn and the need to avoid overgeneralizing.

"Partners! Readers!" I got their attention. "Let me summarize what I heard you saying. First, both Eliza and Thomas noticed important historical details in the book—well done! You'll want to mimic that work—read, really zooming in on details that teach you new ideas and information.

"But many of you noticed that Eliza made sweeping statements about *all* people. That's the *overgeneralizing!* That means assuming that because you learn about one character's experience in the novel, that everything and everybody in that time period was *just like that*. You should be asking, 'Who are we really talking about? Did everyone eat lots of butter then?'

"Thomas, on the other hand, was more specific, accurate, and careful. That's the way you want to be. He even noticed that it was families like Annemarie's who had been accustomed to cream and butter who now missed having it. He knew there were probably people in Denmark, long before then, who didn't get to eat cream!"

ACTIVE ENGAGEMENT

Channel students to make their own similar notes, this time working with a passage from *Number the Stars*.

"Let me give you a quick chance to try this work together, so you can compare what you learn, and make sure you are being more like Thomas: specific, accurate, and careful. I'm going to read two pages from *Number the Stars*. It's the part right after Annemarie brings the basket to the boat, and then her uncle takes her into the barn and explains what happened.

"Can you do the work that Thomas and Eliza did, jotting a bit of what you learn here? Both information, and also what you learn about people's perspectives? Only as you do this, be careful to not overgeneralize. Use phrases like 'People who . . . seem to have . . .' and 'Some people. . . .' After I'm done reading, you and your partner can compare."

I quickly read the excerpt from Chapter 16, "I Will Tell You Just a Little":

> [Uncle Henrik is speaking here.] "Many of the fishermen have built hidden places in their boats. I have, too. Down underneath. I have only to lift the boards in the right place, and there is room to hide a few people. Peter, and the others in the Resistance who work with him, bring them to me, and to the other fishermen as well. There are people who hide them and help them, along the way to Gilleleje."
>
> Annemarie was startled. "Peter is in the Resistance? Of course! I should have known! He brings Mama and Papa the secret newspaper, *De Frie Danske. And he always seems to be on the move. I should have figured it out myself!"*
>
> "He is a very, very brave young man," Uncle Henrik said. "They all are."
>
> Annemarie frowned, remembering the empty boat that morning. "Were the Rosens and the others all there, then, underneath, when I brought the basket?"
>
> Uncle Henrik nodded.
>
> "I heard nothing," Annemarie said.
>
> "Of course not. They had to be absolutely quiet for many hours. The baby was drugged so that it wouldn't wake and cry."

There was quiet as the children read and jotted. Then gradually, they began to compare what they had learned, mentioning the secret newspaper, the compartments in fishing boats, and so on.

Recap the moves readers have made, as they read to learn.

"Readers, I can hear you being more careful. You did say things like 'Children like Annemarie might not have known about the Resistance' and 'A lot of Danes, like Uncle Henrik, admired the Resistance.' But you didn't claim that all the Danish admired everything the Resistance did."

LINK

Send children off to read, suggesting that "reading to learn" is an important addition to their repertoire of strategies.

"My point today, readers, is that you can always learn history from historical fiction stories. But to do that, you want to remember that historical fiction novels can give you powerful glimpses into *some* people's perspectives on a historical

When helping children to think about the particular perspective they've been let in on, help them to notice that a person's perspective on the world reflects not just his or her personality but also the role she or he plays in society, the person's age, race, religion, group membership, and so forth.

event, but it's not *everyone's* perspective. You can also learn about history from biography, as you know, and again, you are learning about the perspective of just one person, or just one group of people.

"Readers, this lesson you've learned today is important in life as well as reading. It's always important not to overgeneralize or make assumptions. So when you go off to work today, you might take a moment to look back over your notes, and see if you want to revise any of your thinking to be specific.

"You can get started reading, but before you do, will you think about our anchor chart, and think about the book you are reading today? Some of you are just in the early pages of a new book, and you are going to want to be thinking about the different timelines in your story—the personal timeline and the historical timeline. I know many of you are reading, noticing parts of the text that seem as if they are written in bold, and you are asking, 'What's this text really, really about?' and coming up with drafts of possible themes. You need to do the work that your book asks you to do at this point in the process of reading it. So before you head off, talk for a jiffy with your club about the work you'll do today, using the anchor chart to remind you of options."

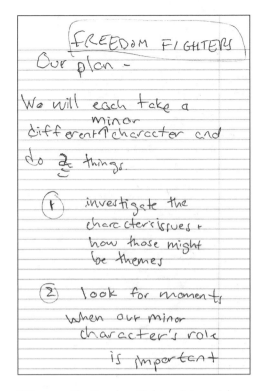

FIG. 14–1 The Freedom Fighters jot a quick plan for their work. It's generally helpful to have kids make a plan before they leave the meeting area—either a group plan or an individual plan. Here, they make both.

ANCHOR CHART

Readers of Historical Fiction . . .

- Read analytically, studying parts that clue them in to the facts, feelings, or setting
- Collect and organize key facts: *who, what, where, when, why, how*
- Keep track of the major character's timeline, the historical timeline, and how they intersect
- Realize that a character's perspective is shaped by the times and his/her roles
- Determine themes and support them with evidence from across the story
- Lodge big ideas in small moments, small details, and objects
- Take into account the minor characters
- Turn to nonfiction to deepen understanding

Moving Back and Forth between Historical Fiction and Nonfiction

Grounding Ideas in Text and in History

YOU HAVE JUST REMINDED STUDENTS to draw on their full repertoire as readers of historical fiction, so you will definitely want to support that. As you confer, ask readers about the work they are doing and nudge them to bring out the relevant tools. If a reader is just starting a new novel, perhaps he is thinking about the character—in which case the relevant strands from the learning progression will help. Readers who are thinking about themes have other tools to guide them.

Remember that you can pull together small-group work that is skill based and not club based. So, for example, if you are finding that some readers are suggesting themes for a book without taking the time to select passages from the text that support those themes, you might call together a small group and remind them that they need to ground their interpretations in evidence from the text. You could ask two readers from one club to work together to find evidence for a theme, marking parts of the text that support their interpretation. Then you could suggest that they reread their suggested passages, pushing themselves to ask, "Which of these *best* supports the theme?"

When you lead small groups, remember that you don't want the conversation to go back and forth between you and one student—like a tennis ball the two of you are playing with. Instead, channel kids to converse with each other, allowing you to listen to one twosome talking, and to coach into their work, then to shift to another, then another. As you shift among children, be sure to encourage students to realize that often when they look to ground their ideas in the exact details of a text, what happens is they realize the wording of the original idea wasn't quite right. Their wording of the theme changes. Celebrate this, pointing out that this is what you meant earlier when you celebrated the way that readers go on journeys of thought. Meanwhile, you may also want to work with students to help a few of them explore the historical trustworthiness of something in their historical fiction. You may want to offer some of them quick research tips to use when they wonder if their novel is historically accurate.

If your classroom has Internet access, you could show students how to navigate one or two Web resources, such as Wikipedia or the American Library Association's history website for kids. Many students would benefit from tips on how to effectively use a search engine. For example, you might teach them that typing in a full-sentence question could lead to a dead end, whereas a key phrase could lead them in the direction of useful answers.

If your classroom does not have Internet access, you might direct students toward printed materials in the room, coaching them to skim with a narrow purpose—to find a specific date, name, or event, and to read around it, to verify, or expand information. However students check their facts, they should add to their notes, using what they find. In addition to indicating whether their initial jotting is fact or fiction, encourage them to record new, relevant information they learn along the way, and to prepare to share with their clubs.

MID-WORKSHOP TEACHING
Characters' Perspectives on Change

"Readers, I want to remind you that just as you want to be careful about overgeneralizing about people in history, you also want to be careful about making sweeping statements about your characters' perspectives. Sam, for instance, was reading *The Gold Cadillac*, and he had been thinking that his character felt invulnerable. He especially pointed to an incident where his character, a black man, drives an expensive car through a white neighborhood. But later in the novel, this character's perspective changes. I won't give away what happens, but Sam is in the Freedom Fighters club, and they're reading about the struggle for civil rights.

"Readers, in a moment you'll meet with your clubs. Will you consider this point when you decide what you want to talk about? Is your character's perspective changing at all?"

Readers Don't Skip the Descriptive Parts

Reading Analytically Means Noticing What Others Might Miss

"Readers, I'm going to admit two embarrassing facts! One is that sometimes I'm bored at baseball games. I just don't understand all the details—like what the catcher is doing, or why it matters, and so I get bored and tune out. Then I wake up and I've missed a whole part of the game! It happens to me with reading too—I get to a part, usually a descriptive part, and sometimes I skip it! It's awful. But readers, after today, I'm going to look harder, and I think you can too. Maybe, just maybe, these descriptive bits are letting us see the world through the character's perspective.

"I'm going to read one of those bits from *Number the Stars*. Will you close your eyes and listen, and think about what this part offers? Does it deepen our understanding of a character's perspective, for instance? Or does it tell us something about how that perspective is changing?"

I read a tiny passage from Chapter 14, where Annemarie described the woods near Uncle Henrik's house:

> *Here the path widened and flattened; it was the place where the woods opened on one side and the path curved beside a meadow at the edge of the sea. Here she could run, and she did. Here, in daylight, there would be cows in the meadow, and on summer afternoons Annemarie would always stop by the fence and hold out handfuls of grass, which the curious cows would take with their rough tongues.*
>
> *Here, her mother had told her, Mama would always stop, too, as a child walking to school. Her dog, Trofast, would wiggle under the fence and run about in the meadow, barking excitedly, trying to chase the cows, that always ignored him.*
>
> *The meadow was empty now, and colorless in the half light. She could hear the churning sea beyond, and see the wash of daylight to the east, over Sweden.*

"Think about it. Can this part teach us anything?" I waited, and slowly, thumbs began to go up around the room.

Listen in to partnerships as they compare ideas, and then have a few share outs with the class.

After giving partners a moment to compare their thinking, I called on a few who had some keen insights. Then I summarized.

"Readers, I heard you saying that Annemarie's mother's perspective has really changed—actually so has Annemarie's. They used to love these woods, and meadows, and find them peaceful and sort of comforting. Now everything seems cold and scary to them. So this bit *was* important. Good thing we didn't skip it! I bet you'll find bits like that in your books, too."

SESSION 14 HOMEWORK

 KEEP TRACK OF WHAT YOU LEARN AS YOU READ HISTORICAL FICTION

Readers, for homework, after you have time to read, find a few parts of the story that feel especially important. They needn't be parts you read tonight.

Then after you have marked those parts, will you think about the work those parts do for the whole story? Imagine that the book is like a Lego castle, and one part is one of the walls. You are asking, "What job does this wall do for the castle? Is it a weight-bearing wall? Does it hold up the roof? Is it just here for decoration?"

The difference is that you will be asking about parts of a story. As you think about the work those parts do, think about what you know about a story's predictable parts. One of those parts might be fulfilling one of these functions:

Introduce the setting	Show changes in the setting
Show the tone of the setting	Introduce a character
Show a character's motivations	Show a character's changes
Show something that influences the character	Show an important event
Show a problem	Show tension increasing, the problem getting worse
Show the character responding to the problem	Show the theme
Show a solution/resolution	

Seeing Power in Its Many Forms

I N TODAY'S SESSION, you'll teach students to consider their stories through the lens of power, including thinking about who has power, how that power is visible, and where there are signs of resistance. Kids love this exercise, although interestingly, they seem to need your help to initiate this sort of work.

We believe critical reading is important because young readers often indulge in a righteous judgment of characters, without really considering the power dynamics of the time and place. For instance, at one point the Freedom Fighters club in this classroom looked up from *Roll of Thunder, Hear My Cry*, shaking with rage. They had just gotten to the part where Mama takes the children to visit Mr. Berry, who has been set on fire by the white townsfolk. I assumed the children were raging against the people who had done this to him. But they were even angrier with Mr. Berry, for not saving himself, and with Cassie's family and the other black families, for "putting up with this." "They should *do* something!" cried the children, entirely frustrated and upset. Sometimes it seems that young readers become confounded by behaviors because they aren't seeing the way access to power is as real as access to a car, a house, or a job. Helping children understand the role that power plays in a story helps them understand cause and effect, tension, motivation, and change.

What's really interesting about teaching children to look at their books with the lens of power is that it leads them to discoveries about the many kinds of power that exist in the world and about the role that resistance can play. When we help readers read with the lens of power, it's as if we help them access whole new ideas and language—and they come pouring out. "Maybe it's not just guns that give power," they'll come to say of *Number the Stars*. "Maybe friendship is more powerful than racism," they'll say as they finish *Freedom Summer*. "Maybe Anne Frank's words have more power than the people who killed her," a child will reflect. They start looking at everything with the lens of power: Who has it? How is it visible? How does it shift? How do people resist?

In the conferring and mid-workshop and share, you remind children to draw on all they know from the unit, to read endings differently—as if they are written in bold—and to begin comparing and contrasting the books they've read in their clubs.

IN THIS SESSION,

IN THIS SESSION, you'll teach your students that readers deepen their thinking by investigating power dynamics in their stories.

GETTING READY

✔ Prior to this minilesson, read aloud Chapter 17 (the final chapter) in *Number the Stars*.

✔ You may want to have on hand some of the timelines, notes, and the excerpts on chart paper telling about when the soldiers stop the girls in the street or come to the house; pull those out, so that you and the children can recall parts of the story where the Germans are the ones with explicit power. Some are available on the Online Resources for this series.

✔ Create a chart titled "Predictable Questions to Investigate Power" with two initial bullets, and be prepared to add to it throughout the minilesson (see Teaching, Link, and Homework).

✔ Be sure you have strands of the learning progressions on hand to use during reading time.

Seeing Power in Its Many Forms

CONNECTION

Tell students that endings of books give us important vantage points and that it is especially important to note surprises, because they can often yield epiphanies.

"So we have finished reading *Number the Stars*. The ending of a book is always a special time. We use that vantage point to think especially about how things fit together—and about things that don't fit, too. We pay attention to bits that surprised us because those bits are often sources of epiphanies, of new realizations.

"I'm pretty sure that as you think back on *Number the Stars*, there are things toward the end of the book that surprised you. Can you think what some of those surprises were?—because remember, they're often worth pondering." I left a little pool of silence. Then I whispered, "There's a part that made my eyes fly wide open. It was when Uncle Henrik told Annemarie that scientists and doctors had worked together to figure out how to make a drug that would confuse the dogs, so they couldn't smell the people hiding in the boats. And *then* he told her that *all the fishing boats in Denmark* were getting those handkerchiefs.

"I'd been thinking that this was the story of one brave family, but now I am thinking, 'Whoa! This is *all of* Denmark!' Resistance leaders like Peter organizing escape routes, fishermen building hidden compartments in their boats, scientists secretly creating drugs, ordinary families guiding friends at night to the boats."

I slowed down, as if thinking aloud a new thought. "Readers, when we started this book, I thought that it was the Germans who had power. They're the ones who made everyone afraid, who took people away, who came in the middle of the night. How many of you felt like I did?" The children nodded vigorously.

"I used to think that it was the Germans who had all the power. But now, I'm starting to not be so sure. There might be other kinds of power."

The children nodded, "Yeah. All the people had more power. It's the power of friendship."

◆ COACHING

This minilesson does not follow the usual pattern in which we first teach readers a strategy or a lens that they can use, show them how to use it, and then scaffold them as they give it a try. Instead, the minilesson starts with the harvest of such work—sharing some of the insights that critical reading can yield.

In this book, Annemarie and her family are not lone agents of change but are part of a bigger movement. Kids can come to realizations such as this, and we help them to grow important interpretive ideas by leaving a trail of bread crumbs.

Teachers, notice that I've just used a version of the thought prompt "I used to think . . . , but now I realize . . ." to convey that my thinking about this story is changing. These phrases have proved to be very helpful to kids, enabling them to recapture their ideas at the beginning or middle of a story versus their ideas at the end.

✿ Name the teaching point.

"Readers, today I want to teach you that looking at our books with the lens of power leads to all sorts of new thinking. When you investigate who has power, what form power takes (how you see it), and how power changes or shifts, that helps you find huge meanings in books."

TEACHING

Share some of the questions critical readers ask, using them to prompt the class in rethinking the read-aloud through this lens of power.

"Readers, there are some questions readers ask to investigate power. At the start of the book, when you are getting to know a new place, it can help to ask, 'Who makes the rules? Who's in charge?'" I jotted those questions on a chart.

FIG. 15–1   Malik's exploration of power

Predictable Questions to Investigate Power
- Who makes the rules?
- Who is in charge?

"Join me, readers, in thinking about those two questions. I'll read some excerpts aloud, and let's think—I'll give you a tiny bit of time to talk or jot, if you want. So, let's see, the story starts with that scene where Ellen and Annemarie dash down the street, and then they bump into the soldiers. Oh, right, and the one soldier gives them orders." I opened the book then, and read aloud in a harsh voice:

> *Go home, all of you. Go study your schoolbooks. And don't run. You look like hoodlums when you run.*

"Let me read on," I said, and again read in a harsh voice:

> *"Where did you get the dark-haired one?" He twisted the lock of Ellen's hair. "From a different father? From a milkman?"*

Then I said, "Share your thoughts."

When children first begin to analyze power, they will see it as a negative force—the force of tyrants and bullies or authority figures. Power to them is all about oppression or domination. In time, you will help them see that there are beautiful, generative powers as well. The lonely strength of those who sheltered Anne Frank. The fortitude of Gandhi defying the British Empire. Harriet Tubman, going back, again and again, to rescue slaves and bring them to safety.

ACTIVE ENGAGEMENT

Add in a new question, to bring students' attention to not only signs of power, but signs of resistance, and set children to trying that question as a lens.

"Readers, I heard you thinking hard about the signs of the power that the Nazis have in this story. Here's another question readers ask. After a reader asks, 'Who has power?' the reader can then ask, 'What's the resistance?' because where there is power, there is resistance. People don't just give in.

"Try using that question as another lens, thinking about signs of resistance in *Number the Stars*. Think for a moment, and when you have an idea, put a thumb up." I waited until thumbs were raised, then motioned for them to turn and talk.

"Readers, I hear you comparing signs of resistance—the handkerchiefs filled with tricks, the necklace clutched in Annemarie's hand, the fake wake for Aunt Birte. You're so right that these show a special kind of power—the power to resist hatred and violence."

LINK

Summarize the replicable process you've led the class through, doing so in ways that could be transferred to other texts and other days.

"Students, do you see that when readers think about stories through the lens of power, it helps to look first at questions such as 'Who has power?' and 'What are the signs of that power?' But then it is also important to ask, 'What is the resistance? What is the power of those who resist?' Doing this, we can realize that there are different kinds of power and that power is not necessarily a bad thing." I revealed the rest of a chart containing questions readers can ask themselves when thinking about a story through the lens of power.

Predictable Questions to Investigate Power

- Who makes the rules?
- Who is in charge?
- Who has the power? What are the signs of that power?
- What is the resistance? What is their power?

"I know you are continuing to ask, 'What's this story really about?' and to draft and revise your ideas about a theme that acts like a big tent idea for your whole book. Think, now, about ways that people use their power in relationships to those big ideas. I know you'll want to talk with your clubs about your ideas. Off you go."

Children are used to seeing the more obvious signs of power: physical force, overt brutality—the power signals of a bully. It's harder to see moral power, because you see it best in its effects rather than in action. All along, in Number the Stars, *the Rosens and the Johansens seem powerless, but in the end, we learn that theirs is a power that is stronger than the power held by the Nazis.*

Consolidating the Year

A S YOU CONFER WITH READERS, you'll want to be sure they are continuing to draw all the teaching you've given them across the unit and the year. To support this, you may want to carry strands of the learning progression with you and be ready to respond to their ideas by showing them where the work they are doing falls on the progression and using the tool to set goals. You may, for example, ask readers to reread the entries they've made throughout the unit, and to select some entries of Post-its that represent their best work on any one of a number of strands of the progression. Chances are good that your students will have written and thought a lot about characters—the aspect of this that will be especially pertinent to this unit relates to thinking about character changes. Fourth-graders are expected to think about how a character changes across a story, and to think about the many causes of those changes. As part of this, fourth-graders also think about what a character learns about life. You can channel children to review entries in which they have done this sort of work (or to make them, if there are none) and then to use the learning progression and their own insights, too, to select one that represents their best work. If a few readers do that alone, you can then ask them to lay their best work alongside each other, compare and contrast, decide which is the best yet, and above all, talk about why.

That same work can be done with many strands of the learning progression. Certainly you will want students to do that work with determining themes.

As you confer today, you'll also probably want to begin asking readers to think across the books they have read throughout the unit. Those books will not necessarily be grounded by theme, but they will tend to be grouped by setting, as most of your clubs were based in a particular historical era. You will want to challenge readers to think between several of their books, thinking, "How are these books similar, and how are they different?" First, of course, you'll hope students engage in freewheeling conversations that uncover some of the really interesting similarities and differences. Then you may want to help them structure their thinking.

To coach them to do this, you might for a moment take two things that are not texts—say, one student's boot, another student's sneaker—and show students how to compare and contrast those. It usually works to start them off saying, "These two

(continues)

MID-WORKSHOP TEACHING
Thinking about Endings as a Way to Think Part:Whole

"Readers, can I stop all of you?" I asked, and waited for children's focus. "There is a lot of interesting work going on in the classroom right now," I said, and quickly summarized the work that students were doing with learning progressions, the intersection of nonfiction and historic fiction, and with comparing and contrasting their club books.

"There is one point I want to make in case you are not in the middle of something—this would be really interesting work if you aren't totally engaged in something else," I said. "As we come to the end of *Number the Stars*, I want to point out that endings of books are special. The ending of a book is like the top of a mountain. You don't want to reach the top of the mountain and then just turn around and race down the hill. Instead, once you are there, you want to look back over the whole trail that you traveled and think about the whole trail in relation to the ending.

"If you have time now—or another time, in your reading life—it is really important to go back to the endings of books, and to reread those endings, and to think about the whole book in relation to the end. You could do that with the endings of any of the books you read during this unit. Reread those endings, and think, 'How does this change my thinking about what the whole book is about?' Think, too, 'How does the ending connect to earlier parts of the book?'"

shoes are mostly the same, but also have differences (or the reverse)." Then they take some traits—say, purpose—and explain how they are the same, starting with the one and going to the next. Then another trait is discussed for similarities—say, basic shape. Then there can be a turn, and now a student says, "Although these are mostly the same, they are also partly different," and again, one difference is detailed, with references to the two shoes. If you do that work for three minutes, you will have set students up with a template to follow as they turn to compare and contrast texts.

Of course, after all that work, it will be interesting to turn again to the learning progressions. Just leave these with the students, asking them to look at ways their work was at fourth-grade level, ways they could revise it, ways they recommend revising the learning progression. You'll find that students can do a lot of this thinking without you there, especially as the learning progression can function as almost another teacher in the classroom.

Readers Pause to Think at the Ends of Their Books

Return to the fact that ends of books are places for readers to pause, to think more deeply, and to think between this part and the whole.

"Fourth-graders, I notice that a few of you have been thinking about the endings in your book, and others haven't yet gotten a chance to do that, so I'm going to ask each of you to pause and do that now. Reread an ending of one of your club books—any one of your books—and for just a minute, think about what work the ending does for the whole book. Ask, 'What work does this part of the book do?' Does the ending illustrate the theme? Does it resolve the problem? Does it introduce a new character, and make you think there will be a sequel?' Try to answer that question, 'How does this part connect to the whole of the book? What work is it doing in the book?'"

I let children work quietly. Then I said, "Will you get together with the rest of your club and talk about what you are thinking? Earlier, we learned that readers pause when they get to parts in a book that feel as if they've been written in bold, they are so important. Endings are almost always written in bold. They're a good time to pause to look back over the trail you have traveled and to do some new thinking. So, do that work now."

As children talked, I moved among their groups, helping them to develop some language for talking about the roles that parts of a book play. I functioned a bit like Johnny Appleseed, telling one club about the sorts of things another club had thought about. I also helped students to talk tentatively, sharing ideas when they weren't exactly sure, saying things like "Could it be that . . . ?" or "I'm not sure I'm saying this right, but I think that. . . ."

CONSIDER THE DYNAMICS OF POWER TO DEEPEN OR REVISE YOUR INTERPRETATION

Readers, for homework tonight, choose an independent reading book that you have finished reading recently—a book that is not historical fiction at all. Go back to that book, and reread a part of it, and try to take all the skills that you have learned during this unit and try them out on that book. Can you think about power in that book? Can you think about the characters whose voices you don't hear? Can you think about why a character's perspective is as it is? Can you think about parts that are written in bold?

Do any of the work that you learned to do in our historical fiction unit, trying to see how much of it transfers to any old book. I think that what you will find is that as long as you are reading a complex and well-written text, the work transfers. I think you'll find we could rename our unit Reading Complex Fiction instead of Reading Historical Fiction.

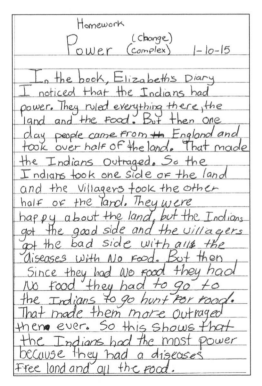

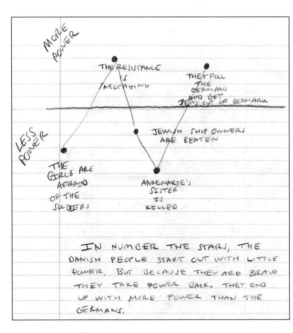

FIG. 15–2

Finding Thematic Connections across Texts

I N YOUR READING AND WRITING COMMUNITY, your children have become at home in the world of ideas. You started by encouraging them to be swept away by their stories, then you asked them to slow down a bit and revisit important parts, and consider how these parts suggested big ideas as they read. Then they opened up the books they were reading, bringing history to bear on them, and read with an awareness of perspective. They're ready to realize that an idea that is true in one book may also hold true in another and that an idea that was embedded in one person's life in the past is oftentimes still relevant today. Universal themes are not actually universal; that is, every theme won't be in every book. But a theme is an idea that is true in many places, in the stories we read and the lives we live.

Today, therefore, you'll invite students to consider how ideas in one book appear in other books. You'll coach them to note the common patterns between books. Students will be excited to note that an idea in one book emerges in another book as well. You can then help students think about the ways a theme can be developed differently in different texts. This work is at the fifth-grade level in the "Comparing and Contrasting" strand of the learning progression. Your children won't master this, but they'll rise to the challenge. Help children perceive that if they reread texts closely, they can notice the same theme is developed differently. Perhaps the primary difference comes from the book being set in a different time or place. Perhaps the characters are very different personalities, dealing differently with a common issue. When teachers piloted this unit, we heard again and again how, more often than not, students surprised them with their ability to do this heady work.

You'll also invite children to take charge of their reading life in a new way. As children begin to recognize themes, they're also ready to conceptualize the notion of text sets. So far, you've organized text sets for them. Sure, they've added in, finding a book here or there that they pursued in independent reading or brought to their club. But in general, you made the basket of books for World War II and for Westward Expansion, and you constructed those text sets according to a historical era. Today's session invites children to organize books by theme rather than by era.

IN THIS SESSION, you'll teach your students that readers look for similar themes across different books to deepen their understanding.

GETTING READY

✓ You'll be working with a big idea generated by one of your book clubs, ideally involving a story that is familiar to your students and an idea that is likely to ring true in other stories (see Teaching and Active Engagement).

✓ Display and add to the anchor chart "Readers of Historical Fiction . . ." (see Link).

✓ Prior to this session, read through the share. You will want to provide at least some books that go together based on theme, along with baskets, labels, and cards on which to write book titles (see Share).

Who knows? They might put *Roll of Thunder, Hear My Cry*, *Number the Stars*, and *Witness* together, noticing that they all deal with the theme of girls learning about violence and choosing to be brave. They might put *Skylark* and *Out of the Dust* with other stories that show humans struggling with the destructive power of nature. But "text sets" can also be a metaphor. Readers don't really have to put books in baskets to enjoy finding ways that books go together. They can picture and talk about books that go together, even if they are not holding the physical books in front of them, or even if they read those stories months ago. In the end, the most important connections will be between the stories in books and those in real life.

"Help children perceive that if they reread texts closely, they can notice the same theme is developed differently."

Finding Thematic Connections across Texts

CONNECTION

◆ COACHING

Explain that as readers get opportunities to talk about books, they are able to layer their thinking about events with thinking about ideas.

"Readers, this whole year long, we've had grand conversations about books. One of the things that has happened over and over is that those conversations have helped us to think in ways that are more layered. On the one hand, you thought and talked about events like 'Annemarie ripped the star necklace off Ellen and then Annemarie held that necklace herself.' On the other hand, you added another layer, and that is a layer of ideas: 'Annemarie was willing to take that risk because she knows friends take care of each other.'"

❧ **Name the teaching point.**

"Readers, you've learned to think hard about people, places, and events in the stories you read—and also about ideas. Today I want to teach you that when you have developed some thinking about a big idea in one story, sometimes that thinking helps you find similar ideas in another story."

TEACHING AND ACTIVE ENGAGEMENT

Ask each club to agree upon a big idea that their book represents, working to say that idea in just a sentence or two. Do some quiet engineering so children word their ideas in ways that will pertain across books.

"Readers, I know you've been doing lots of idea work with your clubs, learning history from stories and grappling with what your stories seem to really be about. I know you've got a bunch of ideas going about each of your books—a bunch of those pink Post-its. I need you and your club to take a second to do the work we have done repeatedly, when you brought your Post-its together to come up with one important, shared big idea for your book and do this with the book you've been reading most recently. Turn and talk with your club, and consolidate your ideas into one big idea that you all care about."

You definitely do not want to suggest that thinking about ideas is superior to thinking about people and plot. In good literature, the plot is never something one discards, leaving just some elevated, abstract idea! Everyone reads great stories for what happens and the people to whom things happen. So just because this lesson shines a spotlight on the fact that readers also think about ideas and themes, you definitely do not want to create some feeling that one way of thinking is higher than another. What is higher, or more sophisticated, is thinking that is layered.

As children agree upon ideas, you'll listen for a club or two that has an idea that you know will turn out to apply to many other books as well as their own. You'll then use that idea in the minilesson—so you'll help that club word its theme so it is easily transferable to other books. Most themes actually are broadly applicable, so this will not be difficult, but you may need to help clubs word their ideas in more abstract ways. Instead of saying, "This is a story about Annemarie learning she could be brave when she had to be," you'll want to help clubs word their ideas more like this: "People can be braver than they realize when the situation requires it."

I invited a club whose idea I had rehearsed earlier, saying, "I'm going to ask the Dust Bowl club to share their interpretation of *Out of the Dust*. They're going to lob their idea over our heads, into the air. It *could* be that their idea fits into one of your books, as well. If it does, then stretch your hands up into the air and pull that idea down to your book." Here I paused, demonstrating how I look up to see this "idea" just over my head, and then reach up and firmly pull it toward my chest. "And then, if the idea fits your club's book, your club will have a minute to say how the idea fits your book."

I got into ready position, hands stretched wide and flexed in anticipation, as if I might just be catching a giant snowball. When the students also looked ready, I nodded to the Dust Bowl club. They shared their theme, which we had carefully worded ahead of time: "One theme in our books is 'People need to find a home, a place where they belong.'"

"Okay, freeze everyone," I called. "Now think, could that idea hold true in your book? If it fits any of your books, grab the idea and swoop it to the center of your club's conversation. Ready?" Across the meeting area, hands reached up, as one child and another scooped the idea that one club had lobbed into the air and convened a conversation around it. Soon children were jabbering about how this theme fit their book. "It's just like Sarah!" Lily exclaimed. "Sarah was trying to feel the prairie was her home," Kobe added. "In *Skylark*, Caleb writes her name in the dirt. He wants her to know it's her home. The prairie is her home."

"Everyone, please look up here. I'm amazed, aren't you? This is an interpretation that the Dust Bowl club developed specifically for their book, *Out of the Dust*. But we lucked out and it went with almost every one of your books!"

I tried another idea, this one from the Allies, who volunteered the theme: "When times are hard, people find ways to survive." Again, club members scooped up that idea and found, with excitement, that it applied to their books.

Talk to the class, suggesting this is no coincidence. The ideas apply across books because these are ideas from real life.

"Readers, what can we make of this? We could say it's a huge coincidence. But I do not think that is the truth of it. And I don't think the authors copied each other's ideas. I think the truth is that when we uncover the deep things that a story is really about, we'll find our big idea isn't confined to just that one book. And the reason for this is that the authors just scooped their idea—as you did—only they scooped it out of *real life*. When you find a big idea—one that is repeated in lots of books by lots of different authors across lots of time periods—here's the big thing: You'll also find it repeated in real life. When an idea applies across lots of books and applies also to real life, some people call it a *universal* idea or a *theme*. This means an idea that could be true almost any place in the universe!"

Bear in mind, teachers, that you already know that almost any idea will pertain to almost every book. But remember, you want the kids to have the rush that comes from discovery. You're fully expecting that there will be lots of hands reaching into the air, and a giddy rush from seeing that "Yes, yes, that idea goes with our book!" And then, from across the room, "Ours, too. It goes with ours, too."

Almost any book yields themes that are broadly applicable. Most of the books the children are reading, for instance, are about how kids grow up rapidly in times of violence, or how danger and hardship can change you. If you've worded your sample theme so it's easy to generalize, as in this case, you'll hear children talk about how Sarah needed a home when she came to the prairie, and how the Watsons were searching for a place to belong, and how Rifka was looking for a home. Don't let too much time elapse before moving to a second theme.

You're acting as if it was just sheer luck that made the first theme universally applicable, although you know that is not so.

LINK

Encourage your readers to use themes as a lens to look across books, and to be open to conversations with other clubs.

"So, readers, our unit is coming to an end, and I know many of you still have books to finish. As you read today, will you be thinking about themes—about the universal ideas that seem to be true across the book you and your club are reading, but perhaps the idea is true across other books you've read in this unit, or even, this whole year? If you have finished your book, instead of starting a new one, spend time getting out books you read earlier and looking across them, and asking, 'Have I read a couple of books that are really about the same idea? How do the messages in these books compare, one with another?' In your club meetings, you'll have a lot to talk about.

"This seems like an important thing to add to our chart as something readers do at the end of a historical fiction book."

ANCHOR CHART

Readers of Historical Fiction . . .

- Read analytically, studying parts that clue them in to the facts, feelings, or setting
- Collect and organize key facts: *who, what, where, when, why, how*
- Keep track of the major character's timeline, the historical timeline, and how they intersect.
- Realize that a character's perspective is shaped by the times and his/her roles.
- Determine themes and support them with evidence from across the story
- Lodge big ideas in small moments, small details, and objects
- Take into account the minor characters
- Turn to nonfiction to deepen understanding
- **Notice universal themes and ideas across books**

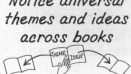

Notice universal themes and ideas across books

Moving from Literal to Abstract Thinking and to Contrasting as Well as Comparing

THERE ARE UNDOUBTEDLY some typical reader profiles in your class. Common among these are readers who love to have big ideas, but they don't love to back them up with real details from the text. Often these thinkers slip into cliché. "It's like all that glitters isn't gold," they'll say. Or, "A bird in the hand is worth two in the bush." At the other end of the spectrum are the kids who have Post-its on every page, and their notes are full of details. They observe everything but construct little from these observations. Interestingly, in both cases, it is helpful to teach and reteach into the relationship between details and big ideas. In this conference, you'll see some moves you can make to help very literal readers begin to make more meaning around details that they notice are repeated in more than one book.

Teach readers to move from noticing details to discerning their significance.

As you approach a club that has two books open side by side, you might ask what the students are working on, and listen to how they articulate similarities between the books. You might even ask them to jot a small T-chart, so you can look quickly for whether the children are noting big ideas or are noticing tiny details that run across both books. When I visited the Allies, for instance, they made a T-chart with *Number the Stars* on the left and *The Butterfly* on the right (see Figure 16–1).

The club could have gone on with this chart, noting other literal similarities for both books—that there was a local resistance movement against Nazi occupation, that Jewish families were protected by Christian neighbors, that soldiers in each book displayed needless cruelty through small actions. You'll want to nudge clubs that are doing work like this away from adding endlessly to a chart of *literal* similarities, however, and check their ability to note *thematic* similarities between the two books.

You might say, "Great work! This graphic organizer helps clarify what you are comparing. Filling out a T-chart is an efficient way of comparing details in books. I have a question, though. Are you aiming to find things that are *literally* similar (like each book has a kitten) or things that are *thematically* similar (like in both books, people find ways to get comfort in hard times)?"

Your question will probably meet with a minute of silence as club members think about this. Then, because they know where you're heading, one will surely say, "Theme." After all, you've been harping on themes lately. "Show me what you mean," you'll prod.

Listen for a moment, then coach in: "May I teach you one thing to help you take your next step?" With their assent, you'll go on: "You've walked me through the similarities between the books. Now, against each of these, you might write out what each

MID-WORKSHOP TEACHING   Common Themes across Books May Be Developed in Different Ways

"Readers, can I stop you for a minute?" I waited until all eyes were on me. "You are doing good work to identify themes in different books. It is exciting to discover themes that are so powerful that they work across many books—and in our own lives."

I paused for a second to signal a slight shift in the direction of my thinking. "But here's another take on themes. It's also interesting to compare how those themes that work across books are actually developed. Sometimes those themes are developed in different ways. For instance, both *Pink and Say* and *Number the Stars* suggest the theme that kids grow up rapidly in times of war. But *Pink and Say* develops that theme through two child soldiers, while *Number the Stars* does it through kids who play a much smaller role or no active role in the resistance movement that adults are involved in.

"So as you compare books and themes, consider how those themes are actually developed. This kind of reading and thinking will add complexity and richness to your understanding of literature."

Number the Stars	The Butterfly
- Annemarie took Ellen's star of David necklace	Sevrine gave her Star of David necklace to Monique
- The girls notice the soldiers tall boots	Monique calls the soldiers Tall Boots
- They took Mrs. Hirsh who owned a button shop	They took Monseur Marks who owned a sweet shop

FIG. 16–1

similarity really stands for. Look at the first one." Point to where the club has written out their first entry, and help them coauthor a theme this detail might suggest. For instance, you might revisit a detail from *Number the Stars*, saying: "Let's take the detail of a necklace, which is in *Number the Stars* and *The Butterfly*. You might ask yourselves, 'What did this necklace mean to each Jewish girl? What did it mean for

her non-Jewish friend? Why did the necklace change hands?' Discuss these a while to see what ideas—or themes—you might uncover that could be true in both books."

Take some notes as the club ponders and debates, then summarize the steps kids just followed. You might say: "Let me name what you just did. You didn't just note the common things that *happened* in each story." I point to the T-chart. "You took something that happened in *each* of these books and you discussed what this might *mean*. And you realized that in each book, it means much the same thing. Let's jot this deeper meaning common to the two books." You're really revisiting a lot of the terrain of the minilesson—but often some students need the extra guided practice of doing this work in the books they are actually reading, with you by their side to provide some scaffolds as needed.

Coach students to contrast as well as compare.

Have an eye toward your stronger readers as well today. These readers may be ready to tackle some above-grade-level work, which is to move from comparing themes that are similar to contrasting how these themes develop in different texts. You might say, "You know, once readers discover a theme that definitely plays out in more than one story, it can be really interesting to investigate how those stories develop that theme differently. Like—are the settings different, so the theme plays out a little differently? Or are the characters different, so that makes a difference? Different authors will have made different choices."

Readers Combine and Recombine Books, Creating Real and Imagined Text Sets

Suggest children consider ways to create text sets of books that go together by theme and orchestrate an opportunity to try this work.

"Readers, I just had a thought. It might be that when you go on into your life, you could decide to put books together into baskets of books that go together by theme, not by historical era. Get with some kids from clubs other than your own, and in the next five minutes, see if you and these other readers can come up with a basket of books that go together. One basket might be 'People are always searching for a home,' and another basket could be 'War makes kids grow up fast.' Get started, and I'll distribute baskets so we can do this for real, and you can make labels for the themes that bring books together. If one book needs to go in several baskets, just write the book title on a card, and stick it in the basket!"

Children swarmed the room, offering up their themes as precious containers. Soon ideas for baskets and their contents were buzzing. As I circulated, I reminded students of books they had read earlier, and gave encouragement when kids suggested movies as well, or biographies, and other nonfiction texts.

"Readers, it is time to stop. I'm glad we have new baskets, new text sets. But readers, I also want to be sure you know that text sets don't have to be real baskets of books that sit in a classroom. They can be collections of books that in our mind we see as beginning to go together. They don't have to be just books, either. They can include nonfiction articles and movies. In your mind and in your conversations, you can think of texts as going together, and just as we've gathered nonfiction facts and stuffed them into our books, we can think of all these books as sort of being pieced together."

I would put Skylark and Out of dust together because the prarie and the no-rain problem are huge in both and they probably have some of the same themes.

FIG. 16–2   Brianna creates a theme-based text set.

Freedom summer and House of sixty fathers should go together because they both have kids who have to grow up fast and they both have kids who do the right thing even when the adults don't

FIG. 16–3   Sam puts two books together, starting a thematic text set.

COMPARE THEMES ACROSS BOOKS AND REAL LIFE

Readers, for homework tonight, continue to think about themes that apply across lots of books.

First, choose two or three books you have read recently, on your own or for class. Write down a few similarities that apply across these books.

Then think about each similarity—what does it suggest in terms of a bigger idea or theme?

After you figure out one or two themes for each book, think across the books. Does one theme apply across these two or three books? Test out that theme. Do the characters, setting, and important details support that theme?

Finally, think about that theme and how it might apply to real life—to your own life or the lives of people you know. What real-life example can you think of that relates to the theme?

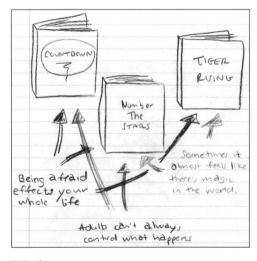

FIG. 16–4

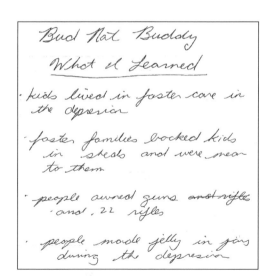

FIG. 16–5

Celebration

Dear Teachers,

You did it! You taught your children to navigate more complex texts, to read more closely, to make their reading into a bigger project, and to fall in love with historical fiction! In this session, you'll celebrate with your students the reading and learning of this unit.

It's important for you to see the significance and power in what your children are doing. The motif of this year has been that we ask students to author lives in which reading matters. We've urged students to spy on themselves as readers, to collect data on their reading lives, to construct reading identities, to aspire toward goals for themselves as readers, and to draw on their growing repertoire of strategies so they can accomplish big work as readers. This final session turns their eyes outward, *toward* the world. The session conveys that we read not because we want to author literary lives for ourselves but because reading enriches our lives. Reading wakes us up. It reminds us of what matters. It helps us to hold onto what is big and beautiful in life. Teachers, we have found a way to live our lives so that we are part of work that is big and important. Our children need the same chance, the same invitation. Reading can give them that. Our job is not only to help kids author reading lives. It is to help them make their way forward, with hope and resolve, with a sense of agency, and a vision of what matters.

You might start today by reminding readers of ways they've marked the end of a unit and celebrated their learning and accomplishments, and let them know that now it is time to honor their learning once again. You might say, "Readers, at the ends of our units of study, we've taken time to make or do things that honor the reading we've done. I've been mulling over what we could do to honor the unit that is now coming to a close. First, I had an idea that we could all dress up as our favorite characters in the historical fiction books we've read and teach each other about the big things those characters taught us, but that felt a little silly somehow, and not big enough to commemorate our work this year. Then it hit me that my problem was that I was trying to come up with one way for all of us to honor what we have learned from this unit and those books, and the truth is, there is not ever going to be one way. The truth is that people need to pause sometimes and think, 'What's important here? What's this really, really about—for me, for my life?' And that is personal work."

Then you might invite readers to create their own celebrations, continue to build their own reading lives, and more than that, become the kind of people they want to be, as inspired, educated, and influenced by texts. Act as if students have been incorporating ideas from historical fiction into their thinking about the world around them. Some have been doing this visibly. But undoubtedly all your readers have had moments when they have thought to themselves, "I wonder how I could make a difference?"

Then you might say something like "So I have decided that each of you, as authors of your own reading lives, will create your own celebration for this unit, capturing some idea that you learned in the course of this unit, that will affect the kind of person you want to be, going forward. This might be a poster, a picture, a poem, a scene you put on with your club. You'll just have today's reading workshop time, so you'll need to think and work fast and furiously."

You might then tell a story of an incident you oversaw, such as a bullying incident, and suggest that you know that your students now would intervene, because they have such a strong sense of justice from their reading. Or you might reread a familiar scene from a favorite book, and suggest students compare how that scene inspires them in the lives they lead. All of this is just to help them jump-start their thinking. Then turn them loose to consider their own books, the lives they want to author, and the way they want to show how they've been inspired. For children who are stuck, you might offer a few ideas. Will they begin a small picture book meant to teach a big lesson? Will they write to a member of Congress, to their mayor, to their principal, or even to their class to suggest change? Will they write a tribute to a brave character in their books? Or will they research a topic they care about deeply (animal rights, taking care of the earth, promoting peace) and begin to imagine the steps they might take to be a part of the change? The possibilities are endless, and nothing is too big or too small for this celebration.

To engage students in sharing at the end of the period, you might orchestrate a quick jigsaw, saying, "Readers, I love the work you've been making. We're going to need to stop. Will you and your club members count off—one, two, three, four? Reader 1s, meet here at the back table. Share what you have made."

You might wrap up today, and the unit, with a little keynote. Call on the great men and women who inspire us to live better lives, saying something like "Readers, these are all brave ideas. Many great activists have talked about how, before you can achieve change, you have to be able to imagine it. Dr. Martin Luther King Jr. talked about having a dream. Gandhi talked about how we need to be the change we want in the world. I think that's what you're doing." Then tell students you're going to gather all their beautiful work and put it on display, so others in your school can see what it really looks like when people are different because of what they read.

Well done!
Lucy and Mary

FIG. 17–1 These letter writers hope to change the behavior of kids who act badly, by showing them that badness, ultimately, is not rewarded.